FRITZ BLANKE

Brothers in Christ

The history of the oldest Anabaptist congregation

Zollikon, near Zurich, Switzerland

Translated by Joseph Nordenhaug

HERALD PRESS, SCOTTDALE, PENNSYLVANIA

DEDICATED TO OTTO SALOMON

IN RECOGNITION OF

MANY YEARS OF FELLOWSHIP

BROTHERS IN CHRIST was originally published in 1955 by the Zwingli Press, Zurich, Switzerland, under the title, *Brüder in Christo*. The author, Fritz Blanke, is Professor of Church History at the University of Zurich.

CONTENTS

On page 32, lines 8 and 9 beginning with "of this memorble week . . ." should read as follows:
the summer of 1525 the time of inner and external dissolution of the Zollikon Anabaptist Church.
Lines 12 and 13 beginning with "of this memorable week . . ." should read as follows:
of this memorable week and evaluate it from the point of view of piety, theology, and sociology.

I

THE FIRST STEPS OF
THE ANABAPTIST MOVEMENT
IN ZURICH (1523-1525)

The preliminary stages of the Anabaptist[1] movement in Zurich consist of five acts, the first of which may be entitled *The Beginning of Estrangement.*

In January, 1523, Zurich became evangelical through an act of the Council.[2] Not all the citizens of Zurich, however, greeted this step with inner assent. Zwingli himself relates that there were in Zurich during that initial period (1523-24) three classes among the evangelicals. The members of one class were merely anti-Catholic, that is, negative Protestants, whose sole "faith" consisted in not being Catholics any longer or not wishing to be Catholics (III, 381,21-383,28).[3] The second class consisted of the libertine Protestants, who saw in the Gospel a charter of freedom enabling them to indulge their own desires (III, 383,29-387,14). From these two groups Zwingli distinguishes those persons who "work in the Word of God" (III, 405,33), that is, the evangelical pastors in Zurich. They did not stand alone; around them gathered a circle of people who really understood the glad tidings. The Zurich Reformer thus assumes a critical attitude toward his own church. He sees her weaknesses, but is grateful to have a corps of faithful fellow laborers who will help him in time to eliminate the defects of evangelical Zurich.

To this group of Zwingli's most intimate fellow fighters belonged also originally Conrad Grebel, the son of a member of the Council, and Felix Manz, the son of a canon at the Grossmünster.[4] Zwingli had shown both of them the way to the Gospel.

How close Zwingli and Grebel once were may be gathered from the fact that one of the most important early writings of the Reformer, the *Archeteles,* closes with a Latin poem by Grebel (I, 327). The *Archeteles* was published in August, 1522.

In the fall of 1523 the first differences of opinion appeared between Zwingli and his disciple Grebel. At first glance they do not seem to be important, yet they carried in them the seed of the later separation. The Council of Zurich had called a meeting for a religious debate in October, 1523, in order to determine, from a Biblical standpoint, what view should be taken of the Catholic mass and the images in the churches. On the basis of what they could learn in this way the Council would in due time come to a decision on retaining or rejecting the mass and images. On the evening of October 27 the discussion about the mass was finished. The conclusion had been reached that the Roman doctrine which held the mass to be a repetition of the sacrifice of Christ was false.

Just as they were ready to proceed to the next theme, Conrad Grebel asked for the floor and demanded that the Council then and there, while they were together, inform the pastors how they should proceed in the future in the practical administration of the Lord's Supper (II, 783,36-784,5). Zwingli replied that the "how and when" of such a decision must be left to the members of the Council (II, 784,6-9). Thus, he was opposed to an immediate measure. In the first place, the Council had not in any way promised such a step when it gave the invitation to disputation (II, 666). In the second place, Zwingli himself had fundamental scruples against proceeding too rapidly. According to Zwingli's opinion the people were far from ready for liturgical changes; they first had to be given

8

more thorough instruction in the Word of God (II, 789,13-14).

Zwingli and Grebel had the same goal, namely the complete elimination of the abuses which had spread under Catholicism. But Grebel wished to abolish them at one blow, while Zwingli was convinced that one must preach "unflinchingly and steadfastly" (II, 788,18-19) against the perverted practices and conquer them inwardly. So Zwingli believed that the Catholic customs would slowly die out under the influence of the new preaching, but Grebel was for quick and thorough action.

Which position was right? Each has advantages and disadvantages. Postponement would make it possible to give consideration to men's consciences but carried in it the risk of procrastination. The sudden abolishment of Catholic traditions, on the other hand, would establish a clear situation, but might do violence to conscience. Behind these two attitudes lie differing traits of character. Grebel was aggressive and incautious. Zwingli thought more in organic terms and was therefore more cautious.

Still another contrast between Zwingli and Grebel became evident in the Second Disputation at Zurich. Grebel demanded emphatically (II, 791,17) that the Lord's Supper be celebrated only in the evening, that instead of the wafer ordinary bread be used, and that each person himself put the bread into his mouth instead of letting the pastor "push it in." These proposals Grebel based on the New Testament (II, 789,26-791,11).

Zwingli remarked that the questions about what sort of bread Christ used at the Supper and whether one should take the bread in one's own hand were not clearly answered in the Bible. Every congregation might therefore hold its own opinion on this point. That Christ observed the Last Supper in the evening was correct, but this time of day for the observance of the Lord's Supper was no longer binding, for if it were, we would still, for instance, be obliged to wear the same kind of clothing as Christ wore at the Last Supper (II, 789,33-792,28).

Let it be said again: Grebel and Zwingli had the same objective; they wanted to carry the Lord's Supper back to its Biblical form. But in doing so, Grebel was more bound to the literal wording of the Bible than was Zwingli. For Zwingli the time of the celebration of the Lord's Supper was an external matter, for Grebel it was not. Zwingli distinguished between essentials and incidentals in the Bible, a distinction which was alien to Grebel. Both were Biblicists, that is, defenders of the authority of the Bible, but Grebel in a narrower sense, Zwingli in a freer sense.

Harold S. Bender[5] speaks of "a tendency to legalism" by Grebel in his understanding of the Scriptures. I hold that to be correct and believe that here again the reason is a peculiarity in Grebel's character. Zwingli called Grebel's urgency at the Second Zurich Disputation "engstiglich" (anxious) (II, 792,22). As a matter of fact, Conrad Grebel corresponds to a psychological type of earnest, pious people with a scrupulous turn of mind, who put a high value on the Bible as book of law—a type which is to be found in all periods of church history, especially in the Pietism of the seventeenth and eighteenth centuries.

We have observed that at the Second Disputation Grebel asked the Council to give the pastors binding directions concerning the Lord's Supper. Thus at that time Grebel still held to the authority of the Zurich Council over the church, that is, to the state church, and therefore of course also to the folk church. Both Grebel and Zwingli were still endeavoring in common to bring about the renewal of the total church of Zurich. At the same time they differed on certain questions. But in the disputation this difference did not yet take the form of an express disruption. Zwingli answered Grebel's questions and wishes calmly and thoroughly. He took his partner seriously. Nor did Grebel contradict the answers given him by Zwingli, and one has the feeling that he was satisfied.

Yet at that time a thorn must have penetrated Grebel's soul. We learn this from a letter dated December 18, 1523, which he wrote to his brother-in-law Vadian in Saint Gall.[6] He wrote that at the Second Disputation the leading theologians of Zurich had set the Word of God "on its head, trampled it under foot, and put it into slavery," and that since then the evangelical cause in Zurich had deteriorated. Why such bitter words? The context shows clearly that Grebel had in mind the mass and the fact that its reformation had been indefinitely postponed at the Second Disputation.

In order to understand Grebel's impatience, it must be recalled that at the time he wrote to Vadian—indeed until Easter, 1525—Zwingli and the other reformed pastors were celebrating the Roman mass (omitting the sacrifice part) in Latin at the altars of the Zurich churches, dressed in chasubles, that they withheld the cup from the congregation, and that Zwingli and his fellow ministers at that time and until Easter, 1525, baptized infants according to Catholic usage with blowing, exorcising the devil, crossing, moistening with saliva, and anointing with oil.

To Grebel this combination of reformed preaching and Catholic ritual was intolerable. He pondered how this half-and-half mixture was to be remedied. And that brings us to the threshold of the second act, whose title is

A Plan that Failed

Grebel knew that the Zurich Council was the main hindrance to liturgical progress. It was therefore essential to attack at this point. The Council would have to be reconstituted; it was to be changed into a body ready for decisive Christian action. To achieve this, Grebel was thinking of the legally prescribed method of a new election.

In order to bring about such an election Conrad Grebel and Felix Manz went to Zwingli and made the following proposition to him (VI, 32-34): Zwingli should issue a proclamation inviting all who wanted to follow Christ to come over to his side. Grebel and Manz were convinced that this call would be heeded by multitudes of Zurich citizens, and that in this way there would come into existence a decided Christian majority. This majority should in turn elect a new Council which would be consciously Christian.

This is the plan of Grebel and Manz. Their objective is to secure a government consisting of believing Council members. Zwingli was selected as the means of achieving this goal. Manz and Grebel knew that all the really earnest Christians had already gathered about Zwingli in Zurich, and they believed that if Zwingli would issue the call, this circle would be considerably enlarged. This was of course not yet the Anabaptist church. No, it is a matter of somewhat tortured church state structure, led by a decidedly Christian government and by Zwingli, to which the majority of the population would belong. There was not yet talk of a new baptism, nor of a minority of believers, nor of Christians not being permitted to be Council members. Grebel and Manz were still searching for the building plan for a new church; they had not yet found it.

We do not wonder that Zwingli rejected this concept of the church. He was opposed to such revolutionary innovation in church and state. He wanted to retain the folk church in the sense of a church for the whole people and to increase the number of believers through unceasing preaching. Zwingli also came to the defense of the existing Zurich Council. To be

12

sure, it did not consist of perfect men, but it did favor the spread of the Gospel.[7]

It was well that the project of the two friends failed. They were then forced to think through their purpose radically, that is, from its root. The result of this deeper testing is found in a long letter dated September 5, 1524, written by Grebel in behalf of himself and his friends in Zurich to Thomas Müntzer in Saxony.[8] The line of reasoning in this writing forms the third act in our presentation and this act will bear the title:

The New Program

First, we encounter again in Grebel's statement the criticism that the Zurich Reformer up to that hour was tolerating the Catholic ceremonies of baptism and the Lord's Supper (14,1; 20,15). We hear that the conclusion, "We must proceed slowly and eliminate the Catholic rites in a forbearing manner," had become a slogan which was worshiped as an idol in Zurich (16,13).

But Grebel did not confine himself to this criticism, which is already known to us. With his confederates he dared to take a step which led far beyond what he only recently had desired. A short time before, he had still agitated for a new form of state church. Now we read: "The Christian church is the congregation of the few who believe and live right" (16,15). So then the Christians remain a minority on earth. From this point on, Grebel rejected the Zurich church of Zwingli; for he considered it a church for everybody, in which timeserving and external belief predominated (13,31).

How the church of the few should be built up externally Grebel did not say. It was probably still not clear to Grebel himself. He does, however, emphasize that the Lord's Supper and baptism should be practiced in the apostolic manner.

13

Every reminder of the Roman mass must be eliminated. In its place a simple Supper was to come, in which only the installation words were to be read, and which would not be taken in the church but in the homes of believers, without clerical dress, with ordinary bread and ordinary drinking cups, as a symbolic meal demonstrating the fellowship of Christians with each other and with Christ (15,12-16,4). Baptism should not be given to children but, according to the usage in the early church, to adults who have become believers, and should signify that we have been washed from sin (17,35-18,41). Baptism and the Lord's Supper therefore [for Grebel] lacked sacramental character.

Those are characteristics of a concept of the church which were not to be found anywhere else at that time. What is the source of this new view of the Christian church? Grebel answers: We were listeners to Zwingli's sermons and readers of his writings (14,6), but one day we took the Bible itself in hand and were taught better (14,8). That is to say, after we had begun to read the holy Scriptures for ourselves, we outgrew Zwingli on certain points (that is, in regard to the church). This is the high self-evaluation of Grebel, who was not a theologian, and of the laymen who had united around him. They were thoroughly steeped in the conviction that they were acting, as Grebel's letter repeatedly states (14,25; 16,7; 17,13; 17, 18; 18,39; 20,31), solely according to the Word, whereas Zwingli did not. This self-confidence is doubly amazing when we consider that Zwingli saw the main superiority of his church precisely in its being built on the Word of God. We therefore stand before the fact that both the innovators about Grebel and their opponent Zwingli simultaneously made the claim of holding exclusively to the Scriptures.

Here too I ask, Who is right? Here too the answer is: We have here to do with two possible but different conceptions of

14

the Scripture principle. The sole validity of the Scriptures means for Zwingli that Christ alone has authority and that justification through faith alone is valid, but that what the Scriptures say about the outward organization of the church, for instance, is not binding. We are, according to Zwingli, bound by the innermost teaching of Scripture, that is by the message of grace, but not by the outward teaching as, for instance, in regard to the organization of the original Christian church. This differentiation does not exist for Grebel and his group. For them the "inner" and "outward" in the Bible are of equal validity. Here we meet the same strict Biblicism which was seen in Grebel at the Second Disputation.

On the basis of their interpretation of the authority of the Scriptures the Grebel circle had the courage to withdraw from the Reformed folk church in Zurich and set out to establish a church form to correspond to the pattern of primitive Christianity, namely, a church of the few who have come to personal faith in Christ and have been baptized on the basis of their faith. In the language of today we call such a group a free church, that is, a Christian fellowship based on voluntary membership and independence of the state.

But Grebel did not preach withdrawal only from the folk church, but also from the life of the state. In the letter referred to, he demanded that "right believing Christians" must not accept public office nor participate in war. This last admonition Grebel directed especially to Thomas Müntzer, who had issued a call to armed uprising by God's people against the ungodly princes. The lot of the Christian is suffering, says Grebel (20,21). Every revolution, every violent act of self-defense, every use of the sword is forbidden to him (17,25-34; 20,6). Here we have one of the earliest testimonies concerning antimilitarism on Christian grounds.

The writing of Conrad Grebel to Thomas Müntzer in Sep-

15

tember, 1524, is the oldest document of the Protestant free-church movement. To be sure, it deals only with the birth of a new thought, not yet with its realization. Grebel proclaimed a principle but did not convert it into deed. So Grebel and his comrades—the very ones who censured Zwingli for his delay—were now also delaying! They had laid hold on a great idea, but they did not at once put it into practice. Perhaps they still felt themselves to be weak in number.

Only twenty men had joined the new movement in September, 1524 (20,19): Conrad Grebel, Felix Manz, Andreas Castelberger, Heinrich Aberli, Johannes Brötli, Hans Oggenfuss, Hans Huiuf, Bartlime Pur, and in addition a dozen others not named (19,19; 21,4). But perhaps they simply did not yet know how and when this new thing which filled their innermost being would take shape. In all the understandable impatience with which they were filled, they did not want to go ahead of God. Therefore, they were prepared to wait. But they did not let their hands lie idle but folded them to pray, as Grebel divulges (14,10). They prayed that God might show them a way out. Surely it is not a bad sign that prayerful waiting stands at the beginning of the Anabaptist movement.

All the men who have just been named had earlier been eager followers of Zwingli. Now the tie between them and their master seems to have been cut. Grebel complained that he and his like-minded friends had been repudiated by the pastors of Zurich (16,30); indeed that they, the "renewers," had been decried from the pulpits as knaves and devils who had disguised themselves as angels (20,24). But on the other hand, we also find in Grebel's letter very harsh judgments on Zwingli and the other personalities in the Reformation. They are accused of arrogating to themselves virtually papal power over the evangelical Christians (21,1). In one place they are even referred to as corrupters of the Scriptures (20,38).

16

Are then the bridges broken? Not quite. And thereby we come to the fourth act:

The Last Attempts at Reconciliation

In the letter to Müntzer the new Lord's Supper had been treated thoroughly, but the new baptism only briefly. And yet baptism soon turned out to be the salient point. For on this point the question of folk church or free church is decided. If only those who have become believers might be baptized, the folk church would be demolished, and also the concept of a state church denied. For at that time in the whole of Europe infant baptism was not only ecclesiastical usage, but governmental decree. It is therefore not strange that the controversy which now begins turns predominantly around baptism. It was also to be expected that the Zurich Council shortly would take a position in regard to this strife about baptism. For already there were fathers—Grebel among them—who for months had not brought their newborn children for baptism.

But even in the last hour, Grebel and his group wished to discuss baptism with Zwingli and the other Zurich pastors in order to convince Zwingli, and if possible through him also to convert the Council to believers' baptism. Zwingli agreed. Appointment was made for private discussions which would be held every Tuesday. Actually only two of these Tuesday discussions were held in the period from October to December, 1524. Others were planned but not carried through, because the parties had quickly moved apart in their discussions.[9] According to Zwingli, the opponents of infant baptism resorted to abuse already at the second conference, because they were bested in the discussion. According to Manz, Zwingli and his colleagues did not give their opponents a chance to speak: "They choked one's speech in his throat," and Holy Writ could not really be listened to.[10]

Since the way through Zwingli to the Council was blocked,

17

Manz turned directly to the members of the Council in writing. His long "accounting" (probably in the beginning of December, 1524) is still extant.[11]

Manz emphasized that he and his friends had thus far kept completely to the course of the final mandate of the First Disputation on January 29, 1523, in which the Council had decided that in Zurich one had to conform to the Bible. But, said Manz, that had hitherto not been done in Zurich in a decisive way (24,1-4). The church ceremonies had not been reformed according to the New Testament. Manz now presents five main proofs to show that infant baptism is unbiblical (24,16-26,24). He hoped that the Council, which had changed its position in regard to church images (26,33), would also be willing to change its conception of baptism. He warned the Council against resorting to any bloody measures in favor of infant baptism (27,15). Finally, he requested that Zwingli present to the Council, in writing, the reasons he had marshaled in support of infant baptism. The Council would then receive a written reply from the Grebel circle (27,18-29).

Zwingli did not compose such a memorial. He did, however, present his proof for infant baptism in a booklet which was published in Zurich in December, 1524, under the title: *Those Who Give Cause for Disturbance* (i.e., for unrest). In this writing[12] he names seven groups of agitators: (1) the merely anti-Catholic evangelicals (III, 381-383); (2) the libertine evangelicals (383-387); (3) the farmers who refused to pay tributes and tithes (387-403); (4) the opponents of infant baptism (403-412); (5) the Catholic bishops (412-420); (6) the Catholic priests, monks, nuns, and abbots (420-423); and (7) the Catholic princes (423-445). We see from this that Zwingli considered the Grebel group as purely religious (not economically determined), and that this group was only one among many which made difficulties for him.

18

Nor was this group around Grebel the most dangerous. According to Zwingli, the controversy with them was in reality not necessary. He restates concerning baptism and the Lord's Supper that the Catholic ritual of both these ceremonies must of course disappear in Zurich; but, he repeats, not by a command from the top but through inner conquest (407,1-15). Zwingli did not abandon this waiting until Easter, 1525. In regard to the differences concerning baptism, church, and the state, Zwingli confesses that he does not hold these themes to be very important. It does after all concern only the outward but not the essential points (404,5; 406,33; 407,21). In other words, Zwingli called out to Grebel that in the things essential to salvation (justification, Christ, faith) they agreed. Why then still wrangle over incidentals? We stand here again before the real cleavage between the two parties, namely, that relating to the range of the validity of the Scriptures.

In conclusion, Zwingli begs Grebel and his associates to work on themselves and get rid of their spiritual pride (407,24-29), but to leave the difficult office of teaching and reproof to the pastors (407,15). That was Zwingli's last appeal for unity. It was not heeded. Zwingli's opponents, as well as Zwingli himself, would have sinned against their consciences if they had retreated. In this way the knot was tied for the fifth act, to which we must give the painful heading:

The Breach

Manz, Grebel, and their circle had demanded a written debate. But this did not come to pass. Instead the Council invited the representatives of the two contending groups to a public disputation in the city hall of Zurich on January 17, 1525.[13] On the basis of Scripture both parties were to present their teaching about baptism. In that way the Council would form its own judgment and then act. But in reality the Council is no longer impartial. For in the invitation the opponents of infant baptism are already designated as the errant ones. So their fate was sealed before the discussion began.

The result of the disputation on January 17 is in fact almost the annihilation of the Grebel group. The Council ordered that henceforth, as before, all children must be baptized within eight days of their birth. Anyone who did not comply with the baptism order of the government would be banished. That is the decree of January 18 (No. 24). On January 21, the Council further decided to prohibit the opponents of infant baptism from assembling (No. 26). Grebel and Manz were forbidden to speak. Röubli,[14] Brötli, Hätzer, and Castelberger were banished, since they were not citizens of Zurich.

How is the brusque attitude of the Council to be explained? I am convinced that they could at this time not act otherwise. They could not allow the centuries-old structure of the Zurich folk church to be destroyed all of a sudden, and to expose Zwingli's reformation, which had just started to flourish, though still threatened from all sides, to new incalculable dangers through the free-church experiment.

The brethren had for a long time prayed God to show them the moment when they must act. Now that moment has come. It was finally clear that it was hopeless to try to win Zwingli and the Zurich government for a re-establishment of the apostolic church; so it is their duty to take the matter in hand. The fellow believers gathered, probably on the evening of January 21, 1525, supposedly in the house of Felix Manz in Zurich. They prayed together, and then Jörg Blaurock arose and asked Grebel to baptize him. Grebel baptized him and afterwards Blaurock baptized the other participants in the meeting. That is the hour of the birth of the Anabaptist movement.

II

THE EMERGENCE OF
THE ANABAPTIST CHURCH IN ZOLLIKON

On Sunday, January 22, 1525, Hans Oggenfuss was leaving the
city. He was a tailor in Stadelhofen by Zurich and had taken
to the road for occupational reasons. Wilhelm Röubli, pastor
in the village of Witikon located high above Zurich, had ordered a suit, and Oggenfuss was taking it to him (No. 31).[1]
The errand required haste, for on the previous day (January
21) the Council of Zurich had ordered Röubli banished because he was one of the leading opponents of infant baptism.
He had to leave the territory of Zurich within eight days (No.
26). No wonder the tailor was striving to complete his busi-
ness before that date.

On the way Oggenfuss became a witness to a strange happening. By the village well of Hirslanden he met two men
whom he already knew. Both were from Zollikon. One of
them was a shoemaker there and bore a family name which
corresponds to his trade, Fridli Schumacher (Shoemaker). The
other is Johannes Brötli, a former Catholic priest, who had at
first gone over to Zwingli. Since the summer of 1523 he had
lived without a parish assignment in Zollikon, and since the
summer of 1524 he had, in contrast to Zwingli, fought against
the baptismal custom of the church. Brötli was living with his
wife and child in the home of Fridli Schumacher.

At the well of Hirslanden both of them stopped, and Schumacher said to Brötli: "All right then, Hans, you have shown
me the truth. I thank you for it and ask you for the sign."

21

Schumacher had received instructions about baptism from his tenant Brötli and had accepted his teaching. But now he desired to take a further step, the step from theory to practice. And therefore he asked for the sign of baptism again, although he had already been baptized as an infant. Brötli without hesitation administered baptism to Schumacher by sprinkling with water from the well.

This is so far as we know the first rebaptism administered to a citizen of Zollikon. It presupposes that Brötli, who functioned as the administrator, had already been rebaptized. Most probably that had taken place on the preceding evening. As already indicated we may assume that the leading opponents of infant baptism—Grebel, Blaurock, Manz, and Brötli—had had themselves baptized in the evening or in the night of January 21 (Saturday). I imagine that Brötli returned to Zollikon from Zurich, where this first rebaptism probably was performed, and that he related this great event to his landlord Schumacher. This may then have aroused in him the desire likewise to be baptized anew.

We may ask why the baptism did not take place in Schumacher's house, where Brötli and Schumacher both lived, but was performed out by the well of Hirslanden. Perhaps caution was the reason. It could be that Brötli, the leader of the baptistically inclined group in Zollikon, considered it advisable to administer outside of Zollikon the first baptism of an adherent from Zollikon.

The gripping thing in this scene is its apostolic simplicity. It is difficult to imagine a greater contrast than that between the baptism at the well of Hirslanden and the baptisms which at that time were customary in the churches of Zurich and surroundings. There, nothing had changed as yet because of the Council's fear of new practices; but the infants were still baptized by Zwingli and the reformed preachers according to

Catholic usage with blowing, driving out the devil, crossing, moistening with saliva, and anointing with oil. But now at Hirslanden all these accessories were lacking, as they had been lacking from baptism in early Christianity.

Just as important to the authors of the Anabaptist movement as the renewal of baptism was the reformation of the Lord's Supper. Already on Sunday, January 22, 1525 (or Monday, January 23), we see Conrad Grebel officiating at a communion service in the home of Jacob Hottinger in Zollikon. Other celebrations took place in various houses throughout the week, partly in connection with baptisms, but also partly without this connection as simply Lord's-Supper gatherings. The procedure was the simplest imaginable. They began by reading one of the New Testament passages about the institution of the Lord's Supper. The reading was followed by a short talk about the meaning of the Lord's Supper, and then they partook of the bread and the wine (Nos. 29, 31, 32).

Let it be said again: The difference between the observance of the Lord's Supper in Zollikon and the manner in which Zwingli and his pastors, in that same January, 1525, celebrated the Lord's Supper is so great that it cannot be bridged. On the altars in Grossmünster, in the church in Zollikon (No. 29), and in all other Zurich churches we still find at that time the monstrance with the host; and before it stands the reformed pastor in chasuble, celebrating the Roman mass in Latin (omitting the sacrifice part), giving the congregation the wafer but not the cup. But here in the farmers' parlors in Zollikon, laymen break ordinary bread and distribute it along with the wine to all participants—a revolution in the history of the Lord's Supper, but, I believe, a necessary and wholesome one!

Concerning the meaning which they attached to these new Suppers we are well informed from the protocols of the hearings. Oggenfuss testified that the Lord's Supper in Hottinger's house was observed with the intention "that they from now on wanted to live and keep a Christian life" (No. 31). Participation in the Lord's Supper therefore implied the obligation to live a Christian life. Jörg Schad confessed that they had broken the bread and eaten it with the intention that "they always would have God in their hearts and think of Him" (No. 31). The Lord's Supper was therefore an obligation to love God!

But still more frequently during this first week we encounter a third interpretation of the Lord's Supper. It is referred to as "a bread of love and Christian disposition," as "a sign of brotherly love and peace," and as an occasion for "showing everybody brotherly love" (No. 31). Eating the bread and drinking the wine together therefore symbolize a mutual fraternal bond; the Lord's Supper is a fellowship meal with evident reference to I Corinthians 10:17: "Because there is one loaf, we who are many are one body."

We feel that in these Lord's-Supper gatherings with their puritan solemnity beats the real heart of the young church. In them they feel themselves to be a holy community tied together by the same bond and united in love of God and their fellow believers.

We raise the question why Zwingli at that time had not already introduced a similarly purified celebration of the Lord's Supper. What prevented him was solely the Zurich Council, to which he submitted. In this regard the Anabaptists preceded him as the first harbingers of the free-church idea, by daring to disregard the state-church institution and by ordering the structure of their church without governmental patronage.

We saw that Röubli, as well as Hätzer, Castelberger, and Brötli, were banished. They had to pledge under oath to leave the state territory of Zurich within eight days, counting from January 21.

Ruedi Thomann, an elderly farmer belonging to a well-known family of Zollikon, did not want to let this time limit pass without seeing two of the banished men with whom he was evidently connected. He invited Röubli and Brötli to a farewell supper (Nos. 29, 31, 32), which took place on Wednesday evening, January 25, 1525, in Ruedi Thomann's house, located in the part of Zollikon known as "Gstad" (Nos. 23-25), today Gstadstrasse.

In addition to the two clergymen and the host, the meal was also attended by Marx Bosshard, Thomann's son-in-law who lived in Thomann's house. While the four men were still eating, Manz and Blaurock entered the room. Ruedi Thomann did not so far know these two men personally. Why did they nevertheless come to him on this evening? Not because of him personally, but because a *forbidden* religious meeting was to be held in his house. Whether this meeting had been initiated by Thomann himself or by Brötli and Röubli we do not know. In any event Ruedi Thomann had placed his parlor at their disposal for it.

After the evening meal three other visitors appeared: Heinrich Thomann, the brother of Ruedi; Jacob Hottinger, an elderly man of one of the best known families of Zollikon; and Hans Bruggbach, of Zumikon, a neighbor village of Zollikon. Nine men—five farmers, three clergymen, and one schooled in secular learning (Manz)—sat around a table, engaged in Bible study. They read from the New Testament and discussed it. What did they read, and what did they talk about? Evidently they considered the human soul to be lost in sin and that according to the holy Scriptures only those who repented and were baptized would be saved.

Suddenly Hans Bruggbach arose. He deplored his sins, yes, he "wept and cried out what a great sinner he was." He besought his friends to pray to God for him and asked them to give him the sign of baptism. This violent outburst of con-

25

viction of sin by Bruggbach can be explained only if on this evening they had talked of guilt and conversion, no doubt in an evangelistic spirit. Bruggbach's request for baptism was granted.

The act of baptism was simple but not without form. The baptism was embedded in a brief liturgy conducted alternately by Blaurock and Manz. First Blaurock asked Hans Bruggbach whether he desired baptism. Bruggbach answered yes. Then Manz quoted a sentence used in a similar setting in Acts 10:47: "Can any one forbid water for baptizing?" Blaurock answered: "No one." Then Manz took a metal dipper ("Gätzi"), the kind which at that time was used in the kitchen, and with it he poured water over the head of the baptismal candidate, saying, "I baptize you in the name of God the Father, God the Son, and God the Holy Spirit."

After the first followed a second baptism in the same meeting. Jacob Hottinger, who during the preceding weeks had proved himself to be a fervent adherent of Manz and Grebel, arose and likewise let himself be baptized by Manz. These baptisms were certainly the main purpose of the gathering. This was not a devotional hour in the usual sense, but a revival meeting which should lead those present to repentance and baptism.

The evening ended with the Holy Supper. Blaurock indicated the bread and wine which were on the table, and broke the bread in pieces. Before he distributed the Lord's Supper, he gave a talk which has in part been preserved. According to the report of Ruedi Thomann, Blaurock said: "He who believes that God has redeemed him through His death and rose-colored blood, let him come and eat with me of the bread and drink with me of the wine." The Supper is therefore, according to these words, a celebration for those who know themselves to be redeemed.

26

The meeting in Ruedi Thomann's home was Bible study, revival, and ritual observance. But it was not least a means to win new members for the baptistic fellowship which had just come into being. From this last point of view the evening was not particularly successful. Two of those present had let themselves be baptized and were taken into the church. But the others? Manz, Blaurock, Röubli, and Brötli had been rebaptized a few days earlier, on or about January 21. There remained therefore three who could not decide to be baptized in this meeting: Ruedi Thomann, Heinrich Thomann, and Marx Bosshard.

About Heinrich Thomann we know that this evening, which according to the aim of the organizers was to have attracted him, rather repelled him. When he saw the baptismal act and the observance of the Lord's Supper he broke out in sweat, as he expressed it, and would have run out the door if he had had to participate. It is the sweat of fear which breaks out of the pores of the old man. No wonder! What he saw must have appeared to this conservatively inclined man as blasphemy against religion. There, a man in a farmer's parlor breaks ordinary bread and distributes it along with the wine. And then a layman performs holy baptism in new and unusual forms, and that on adults who already have been baptized!

Heinrich Thomann was, however, the only one for whom the meeting on January 25 became weird. Probably he was inwardly distant from the circle. Perhaps he had come only through curiosity into this pious fellowship. His brother Ruedi was close to the Anabaptist movement, otherwise he would not have invited Brötli and Röubli.

Marx Bosshard is also touched by the new movement. To be sure, Bosshard could not on that evening decide to be baptized, but what he had experienced kept prodding him. After the

27

visitors had taken leave—only Blaurock and Manz remained with Thomann for the night—Marx went to his room. But he could not sleep. During the night it "kept attacking him," as he expressed it; that is, he remained disturbed. He did not know any other way out than to ask God to give him the correct insight. Toward morning the understanding he had prayed for broke through with convincing power. Now he knew: You must be baptized.

He arose very early on Thursday morning, January 26, and awakened his father-in-law as well as Manz and Blaurock. Between the young farmer and Blaurock a conversation developed about personal spiritual matters. The main content of the conversation has been preserved by Ruedi Thomann who overheard it. Blaurock said to Marx: "You have hitherto been a gay young man," and exhorted him (on the basis of Ephesians 4:22-24) to put off the old Adam and put on the new and repent. Bosshard was ready to do so. After he had ascertained his willingness to repent, the chief condition for baptism, Blaurock could baptize Marx Bosshard. Already the same year we meet Boshard as an itinerant Anabaptist preacher in the upper territory of Zurich.

Now it was Ruedi Thomann's turn. So far he had hesitated, but Blaurock pressed the matter home to him: "You are an old man and near death. You, too, must repent and ask for baptism!" Ruedi is willing, and Blaurock added him also to the church. So the circle was complete. All participants in the meeting of January 25 have now received the sign of baptism, with the exception of the outsider Heinrich Thomann.

But such a man as Blaurock is not satisfied with that. Is it not recorded in Acts 16:33 about the jailer in Philippi that he and all his household were baptized? And must not a society of baptistically minded people, who want to renew the original Christian pattern, also take this feature into account?

This is Blaurock's reasoning, and consequently he urged Ruedi Thomann that he should also have his family and servants baptized. Thomann agreed, and so on this January morning the farmstead in Gstad became the scene of another group baptism copied from apostolic usage.

Two days later, on Friday, January 27, 1525, another gathering was arranged, also in Gstad, but this time in the house of Hans Murer (now Bahnhofstrasse 3). Brötli led the meeting. His departure was imminent. Among the participants we know the names of Heinrich Thomann, Lienhard Bleuler, Conrad Hottinger, and Hans Bruggbach's son from Zumikon. Brötli had the joy of seeing the three last-named men apply for baptism, which he performed at once by pouring water over them. Also this time Heinrich Thomann remained unrepentant. Later he declared that he felt as though "his hair stood on end" when he witnessed the baptism of the three men by Brötli (No. 29).

We know further about a meeting in the house of Felix Kienast (today Rütistrasse 43), where Felix Manz baptized farmer Jörg Schad and others; but it is not now possible to determine on which day of the week between January 22 and 29 it took place (No. 31). Evidently gatherings were held every day, particularly in the evenings (No. 29). Most of the baptisms were administered by Brötli, others, as we have seen, by Blaurock and Manz. Rudolf Hottinger admits that he baptized one young woman who with tears had begged him to do so (No. 33).

Conrad Grebel, who already at the beginning of the week had left for Schaffhausen, evidently did not baptize anyone in Zollikon.

So far we have followed the events through Friday. Two days later, on Sunday morning, January 29, the churchgoers in Zollikon experienced an unpleasant incident (No. 29). They have gathered in the church for worship. Their pastor, Niklaus Billeter, is about to mount the pulpit, when a man in the audience arises from his pew and steps in his way. We recognize him by his black hair, his bald spot, and his blue suit as Jörg Cajakob, called Blaurock (No. 109).

Between the two an excited conversation takes place before the congregation. Blaurock asks the pastor the rhetorical question of what he intends to do. Billeter answers as a good Zwinglian: "I will preach the Word of God." Blaurock replies: "Not you, but I have been sent to preach." Billeter calls his attention to the fact that *he* has been sent, namely, by his superior at the canon seat of the Grossmünster Church in Zurich, which for ages had engaged the clergyman for Zollikon.

Blaurock was not satisfied by this information and continued to talk. Meanwhile, Billeter had mounted the pulpit and had begun to preach. But Blaurock was still disturbing, and Billeter interrupted his sermon, came down from the pulpit and turned toward the door, certainly not to vacate the place in the pulpit for the disturber but to shorten the tumult. But Billeter had figured without the congregation. Some of those present were not agreed to his retreat and called to him to remain. So Billeter entered the pulpit a second time and continued his sermon. He warned the people against disturbance and asked that if anyone wanted to show him his errors he should do so privately in the parsonage, but not here in the church—certainly a request which one must approve.

Blaurock felt himself hit and interrupted the sermon anew. He called out to him the words from the narrative about the cleansing of the temple: "It is written, 'My house shall be called a house of prayer'; but you make it a den of robbers." Blaurock had a stick with him, and the inner passion with which he poured forth these words released itself in three or four blows with the stick on a pew during his outburst.

But that was now enough. Deputy Bailiff Wuest, who was present in the church, arose and threatened the disturber with jail if he did not immediately desist. Now Blaurock became quiet and the incident was closed.

What did Blaurock really want? He wanted to do in Zollikon what he succeeded in doing in Hinwil in the upper territory of Zurich six months later. There on October 8, 1525, the people had come to the regular Sunday morning service of the church and awaited the pastor. But before he (Hans Brennwald) appeared, that is, before the service began, Jörg Blaurock stepped up into the pulpit and preached, introducing himself with the explanation: "Whose house is this? Is this God's house where the Word of God should be proclaimed? Then I am here as an ambassador from the Father to proclaim the Word of God" (No. 109).

A usurpation of the pulpit! Brennwald came too late; he was not able to expel the intruder and had to call on the bailiff for help.

In Zollikon, too, Blaurock had doubtless wanted to seize the pulpit. But here he had no success because the pastor was already present. Why he had aimed at the pulpit seems clear to me. For a hotspur like Blaurock, the development of the Anabaptist movement in Zollikon was too slow. He wanted to attempt to convert the population, if possible, at one stroke through preaching in the church. The authority for it he drew from his highly intensified sense of mission. He felt himself to be a prophet with a direct calling to spread the Word of God and cleanse the temple of God.

But the test of strength failed in Zollikon. Blaurock could not deliver his message to the people. On the contrary, through his forwardness he planted the seed of the downfall of the Zollikon Anabaptist congregation. For, through the incident in the church, the state authorities saw themselves induced to

31

step in. On Monday, January 30, 1525, the city police appeared in Zollikon and arrested Blaurock, Manz, and all the farmers who had been baptized in the past eight days (No. 29).

With that event the eight spring days of the Anabaptist church of Zollikon were over: I mean the days of the first undisturbed development. The time of government pressure, fines, and imprisonment had come. Thereupon followed in of this memorable week and evaluate it from the point of view of piety, theology, and sociology.

Having shared in the events which took place in Zollikon on January 22-29, 1525, it remains that we make a cross section of this memorable week and evaluate it from the devotional, theological, and sociological point of view.

When we seek a caption for the inner processes of these eight days, the concept "revival movement" presents itself. We thereby understand the sudden occurrence of a religious awakening, in which not just a few individuals but a considerable number are gripped by a personal Christian disposition to repentance and break through to the joy of salvation.

This happened in Zollikon. We can still clearly see the process of repentance in sequence from the protocols of the hearings (Nos. 29, 31, 32). It starts when the consciences of individual persons begin to beat and they become disquieted because of their sinfulness. The next step is that they implore God for full conviction of sin. Then follows the break-through of this conviction; their own guilt and sin are uncovered before them.

It is striking how deep this consciousness of sin reaches. Conrad Hottinger realized that he was a great sinner and that no sinner could be saved. Hans Bruggbach expressed himself in a similar way. Jörg Schad came to the conviction that he had spent all his days running around in vice and sin. Thereby they certainly do not think of individual sinful deeds. But these men, who have hitherto lived as upright citizens and members of the church, become conscious that their whole past life cannot stand up before the absolute judgment of God, and that they are under condemnation because of original sin. Here we meet the reformational understanding of sin, and that not just as abstract theory but as personal experience.

The impact of this experience is underscored by the strong emotions accompanying it. These farmers, who otherwise certainly were accustomed to hide their feelings, broke out in loud wailing and weeping.

The way of conversion in Zollikon has, however, still two other stations. From the depth of their agony of sin rises the cry for salvation, for "cleansing and forgiveness of sins," for "the grace of God." But the one crying for help knows that he may expect the forgiveness of God only when he is willing henceforth to cease from sin. Jörg Schad confesses that he has acknowledged his sins through the grace of God, and knows that "if he would abstain from sin," God would forgive him.

Forgiveness is experienced in baptism. Baptism makes an end to the "struggle of repentance" and brings release from the heavy load of sin. For it is regarded as the visible sign that God has pardoned the sinner. Blaurock asked the men in Ruedi Thomann's house if they desired the grace of God. When they said yes, he baptized them. Baptism is a sign of grace.

But baptism has still another meaning. Rudolf Breitiner, shaken to tears by his burden of sin, declared to Brötli that "he would from now on abstain from all his sins, and as a token of this he should baptize him." Breitiner therefore was willing henceforth to say no to sin, but in order to carry out his intention he needed baptism. Baptism is here evidently regarded as the divine assent and confirmation of the human resolution.

Similarly we hear from the mouth of Jörg Schad that "he

requested the sign of brotherly love, that he would do good unto his neighbor as to himself, and that he let water be poured over him." Schad wanted to begin a new life and in the future live according to the standard of the Sermon on the Mount: "All things ye would that men should do unto you, even so do ye also unto them" (Matthew 7:12). But for that he needed the sign of baptism as a sign of brotherly love, that is, as a sign which makes brotherly love possible.

Therefore baptism has a double significance in Zollikon. It affirms that God gives the penitent grace, and that He bestows on the forgiven person the power to walk in newness of life.

What we observe in the farmers of Zollikon is therefore a complete and unified process of inner change. These occurrences have in them what we always see in revival movements, an irresistible and eruptive character. When the judge asked Hans Bruggbach why he had let himself be baptized, he answered: "It had struck him in such a way that he simply had to do it."

For Rudolf Breitiner the sense of sin did not erupt in a meeting but under the open sky just as he came to the Nebelbach on an excursion with Brötli and Felix Kienast. He stopped and began to weep and wail over his sins. Meanwhile Brötli had gone on. Breitiner called him back and asked to be baptized.

We are familiar with the criticism which Goethe made of the writing of church history. In the ninth of his *Zahmen Xenien* he says: "What do I have to do with church history? I don't see anything but parsons. How it goes with the Christians, the ordinary people, about that I can find nothing." In reality, the sources of church history do show us how the theologians have felt and thought, or what great personalities have deeply experienced. But of the soul struggles of the or-

34

dinary, nameless Christian man we hear practically nothing. The protocols of the hearings, which are available to us in connection with Zollikon, form an exception here. Here we can look into the hearts of plain men of the people and participate in their spiritual fears and joys.

It is not only the Zollikon texts that are extraordinary but also the matter which they contain. From the period of the Reformation I know of no revival events like those told us from Zollikon. Above all, I have nowhere else encountered this almost stormy eruption of the spirit of repentance which grips an entire group of people.

Such a unique movement of repentance must be explained. Having thus far considered its external and inner course during the first eight days, we must now inquire about the stimuli which in the last analysis precipitated it. I want to distinguish between the theological and personal impulses.

It can be demonstrated that Conrad Grebel and his circle of Zurich opponents to infant baptism had already in the year 1524 come to the conviction based on the New Testament that repentance must precede baptism (No. 14). Unrepentant people must not be baptized. They assumed that the person to be baptized must have reached an age at which he is capable of repentance. Only adult, repentant persons could therefore be baptized.

In the beginning, that was just doctrine. It became practice around January 20, 1525. At that time adult baptism was introduced in practice. That meant that the people who wanted to be baptized again were told: You must first repent, that is, you must be converted. Personal conversion or repentance was now given decisive weight as the necessary antecedent of baptism. Without repentance, no baptism, that is, no redemption.

Behind the Zollikon revival stands a new doctrine of repentance which is the theological motive of the movement. But the real impulse was given by the revival sermon which developed from this doctrine of repentance. The religious stir which we have just examined was set in motion because there appeared in Zollikon personalities who with authority sounded forth the call to repentance.

We know the preachers: Grebel, Manz, Brötli, and Blaurock. Among them Blaurock (Jörg Cajakob) is the outstanding figure. He was the son of Rheto-Romanic peasants in Bonaduz in the Grisons.[2] He became a Catholic priest in Trins. About the year 1523 he broke with his old faith and became a Zwinglian. He married the same year. We see him in Zurich for the first time as he appeared for the discussion of baptism on January 17, 1525, where he fought against infant baptism. He must at that time have been about thirty-three years old.

Blaurock was a hothead. His friends called him a "second Paul," meaning that piercing apostolic power dwelt in him. Today we would probably call him an evangelist. We have seen how urgently he spoke to the consciences of Marx Bosshard and old Thomann, and how he pressed Ruedi Thomann to let himself and his family be baptized. Blaurock was dynamic. The revival movement in Zollikon must be ascribed in the first place to his evangelistic initiative.

That Blaurock did not lack vehemence is apparent from the "tempest" in the church of Zollikon on January 29. This occasion was, to be sure, an argument with a hostile pastor. Whether Blaurock's preaching in the meetings or his private counseling also had something of a violent character we do not know. But it is possible. Many may simply have let themselves be carried away by the temperament and power of suggestion of this pusher.

Ludwig Keller maintained in his formerly extensively read works that there is a close historical connection between the

Anabaptists of the Reformation period and the Waldensians and other "sects" independent of Rome in the Middle Ages. This was particularly true of his work *Die Reformation und die älteren Reformparteien*[3] (Leipzig, 1885). He considered the Anabaptists merely the perpetuators of the medieval extra-church movements. Occasionally we encounter this opinion even today.

A good method is available for clarifying this old problem. We can investigate whence the theological foundations of the Anabaptist movement in Zollikon came. The Anabaptist church of Zollikon was the oldest in existence. If anywhere, it should be possible to show from the theological attitude of this church whether the Anabaptist cause was born of the Middle Ages or of the Reformation.

Let us briefly review the separate tangible points of this emergent baptistic theology in Zollikon during the week of January 22-29. Jörg Schad and Marx Bosshard report that they prayed to God for conviction of sin (No. 31). They knew then that not only the forgiveness of sins is a divine gift, but that conviction of sin is a prior divine gift. This is what Zollikon Anabaptists and especially their leaders had learned from the message of Zwingli. So much the more had they drawn from Zwingli their consciousness of the total depravity of unregenerate man; likewise their knowledge that redemption is based on grace alone. The doctrine that the way of salvation from the very beginning stands under "grace alone" is the decisive Reformation discovery, which also dominates the Anabaptists of Zollikon, whereas the Middle Ages, including the Waldenses, knew nothing of it.

In the matter of the sacraments the Anabaptists of Zollikon were the pupils of Zwingli, in so far as they understood baptism and the Lord's Supper symbolically and not sacramentally (in contrast to Catholicism and Luther). For them the Lord's

37

Supper is a symbol of the brotherhood of Christians and not an offering of the body of Christ. Baptism does not mediate the forgiveness of sins, but is a sign indicating that God has forgiven the believer.

But Zwingli's influence is still more evident in the way in which, for instance, the rebaptized farmer Lienhard Bleuler describes his relationship to God and Christ. When the judge asked him if he in the future would renounce the practice of rebaptism, he answered that "he is God's servant and no longer has might and power over himself, and has enrolled under the Captain Jesus Christ and will go to death with the same, and what He commands and enjoins him, he will obey and do it" (No. 33).

These are to the last detail Zwinglian formulations. Christ the captain in whose troops we have enrolled, for whom we shed our blood and who gives us His Spirit—this is a frequently recurring picture by Zwingli. Bleuler lived completely in this concept. He said to the judges: I can no longer dispose over myself, for I have become a soldier of Christ, from whom I receive my orders. If it must be, I will go to death for my Captain.

Rudolf Hottinger expressed himself in a similar way. He knew himself to be a servant and slave of God, and must "listen" and bide what God's Spirit would show, teach, and bid him (No. 33). This feeling of the Christian's exclusive dependence on God's command is the kind of Christian self-evaluation Zwingli taught. Rudolf Hottinger and his friends had no doubt originally been especially faithful followers of the Zurich reformer, for they understood well Zwingli's point of view concerning the Christian position. But now they applied the consciousness of personal guidance from God, which they owed to Zwingli, against Zwingli and his conduct of the church.

From the conviction that they could know themselves to be servants of God and soldiers of Christ, the men of Zollikon derived a consciousness of independence of the Zurich church, and also of the state. Rudolf Rutschmann confessed in his own name, and in behalf of the fourteen other Zollikon farmers who were his fellow prisoners, that "he had let himself be baptized. And since he is a servant, slave, and obeyer of God, he will also do what God's Spirit instructs, teaches, and commands him. And therefore he will defer to no one, nor will he let himself be dissuaded by any worldly power. Otherwise he will be respectful and obedient toward his honorable masters of Zurich in everything which is not against the will of God" (No. 30).

Who cannot perceive the Reformation spirit in this courageous declaration by the fifteen winegrowers of Zollikon? Luther had said something similar in Worms. And Zwingli, too, particularly in his earlier years, had basically rejected the interference of the government in matters of religion and conscience, especially so far as Catholic states were concerned. He now must experience that this same demand is made by Zollikon of the evangelical government in Zurich.

But so much is certain: the soil in which grew the new thinking of Grebel, Manz, Brötli, Blaurock, and their followers, was not the Middle Ages, neither the Roman nor the Waldensian, but Zwingli's reformed teaching. The earliest Anabaptists had all gone through Zwingli's school and absorbed the basic items of the evangelical faith, which they could never forget.

But did these disciples nevertheless not turn away from their master? Certainly. They placed repentance before baptism, they baptized adults, they emphasized that baptism also means power for a new life, they observed the Lord's Supper as a fellowship meal, and they rejected the state church and the folk church.

These were the differences in the year 1525 between the Anabaptists and Zwingli. But what is the direction of these differences? Did the Anabaptists want to go back to the Middle Ages and seek to revive them? On the contrary! They desired, with deviation from Zwingli's line on certain points, to carry forward the Reformation; they wanted to continue building on the foundation laid by Zwingli. The deviations from Zwingli go in the direction of a more literal, even stricter adherence to the Holy Scriptures. The authority of the Bible is the guide for Zwingli as well as for the Anabaptists who went out from him; but in the application of this guide in particular matters the Anabaptists thought more literally, more Biblicistically. Thus arises the contradiction between the teacher Zwingli and his ultra-Zwinglian disciples. It may be said that Anabaptism, precisely through this distinction of reference solely to the Bible, was a daughter—self-willed, to be sure—of the Reformation.

Still another question awaits answer. Was the awakening in Zollikon of genuine religious nature, or was it also conditioned by political and social influences? How far economic conditions were involved in the rise and spread of the Anabaptist movement has not been sufficiently illuminated. We will now seek to find an answer to this question with respect to Zollikon.

Zwingli accused the Anabaptists of Zollikon of having communistic tendencies: "These cursed people want the goods of those in poor circumstances to be shared in common, but their own, so far as they have any, not at all."[4]

In support of this assumption he cites a weaver by the name of Heini Frig, called "Gigli," in Hirslanden by Zurich, who had told him that the Anabaptists of Zollikon had eaten up his winter supplies.[5] We meet this Frig also in the court hearings. He had let himself be baptized in the week of January 22-29, and was arrested along with his like-minded fellows on January 30. In contrast to the other Anabaptist prisoners he very quickly deserted his stand and in the bargain accused his former friends of a tendency to communism. He testified that he had been pressed by the Anabaptists of Zollikon to sell his small farm and give up his trade. The plan was that all things should be held in common and everything be pooled in one treasury, from which all were to live.

Here Frig goes further than he had before Zwingli. Which of the two statements is nearer the truth? May he be considered a dependable witness? Caution is in order, since his assertion stands quite alone. Not a single official document confirms it. Besides, the Zurich officials themselves evidently did not take his report seriously. For among the questions which were put to the imprisoned Anabaptists of Zollikon in 1525 by the judge who conducted the hearings, the question about community of possessions is lacking, in spite of the fact that Heini Frig had made this serious charge at the beginning of the year. Under these circumstances we may, I believe, seriously question the existence of any communism in Zollikon.

The number of persons whom we know to have been baptized in Zollikon between January 22 and 29 was about thirty-five. Among them was one woman. Thirty-four were men. Rebaptism was in this first week the concern of men. Among the thirty-four were four servants. That leaves thirty self-employed farmers. They belonged to the old resident Zollikon families of Breitiner, Bleuler, Hottinger, Kienast, Murer, Rutschmann, Thomann, and others. The Hottingers are represented by the greatest number.

Concerning the economic position of the farmer families involved in the Anabaptist movement we are indebted to Heinrich Bruppacher for his investigations,[6] which were confirmed by Paul Guyer.[7] Zollikon had about fifty big farmers and about forty small farmers. The Anabaptists were preponderantly in the latter class. Some of the wealthier families were not represented at all among the Anabaptists, such as Brunner, Ernst, Falk, Häusler, and Obrist. On the other hand, of the forty small farmers, the majority—nearly thirty—were seized by the Anabaptist movement.

May we interpret this evidence to mean that economic factors played a role in the Anabaptist revival of Zollikon? That depends on the economic circumstances of these small farmers. If they were poor, they might have expected an improvement of their situation through the Anabaptist movement. But according to Bruppacher, "They are not particularly among the poor, but they are making a good, honest living by supplementing their small-scale farming through working as day laborers or at a trade."

It is of course striking that the well-to-do circles held back, while the people living in humbler circumstances participated in the revival. But is it so different today in regard to the participation of different classes in the life of the church? This ratio has nothing to do with economic aspirations.

That social hopes played a part in the Anabaptist movement of Zollikon seems completely unlikely in the light of the severe inner struggle which preceded the conversion of each individual, the terrors of conscience[8] which these men passed through. These small farmers were not concerned about money and possessions but about their guilt before God and about liberation from this guilt.

In the emergence of the Anabaptist church of Zollikon we have to do with the birth of a community of purely religious character.

42

III

COLLISION WITH THE·AUTHORITIES

On Sunday, January 29, 1525, Johannes Brötli, the first leader of the Zollikon Anabaptist congregation, had started on his way to exile. His last word was a warning to his like-minded friends who remained in Zollikon. He warned against apostasy (No. 36). His concern is understandable. It was only eight days since the Anabaptist fellowship had come into being, the very first of its kind. It was clear that its testing still lay ahead.

On Monday, January 30, Felix Manz and Jörg Blaurock were arrested in Zollikon, along with the following twenty-five local men: Hens Bichter, Lienhard Bleuler, Marx Bosshard, Hans Bruggbach, Uli Bruggbach, Rudolf Breitiner, Heinrich Frig, Valentin Gredig, Hans Hottinger, Heini Hottinger, Heini Wisshans Hottinger, Jacob Hottinger, Conrad Hottinger, and his son Rudolf Hottinger, Rudolf Hottinger (in the upper village), Felix Kienast and his son Hans Kienast, Ritz Keretz, Grosshans Murer, Hans Oggenfuss, Rudolf Rutschmann, Jörg Schad, Fridli Schumacher, Jacob Unholz, and Hans Wüest (No. 38).

The legal reason for the arrest was obvious in the case of Manz and Blaurock. Since January 21, Manz had been under injunction not to speak. This order he had violated. Blaurock had on January 29 disturbed the public worship in Zollikon. In addition, both men had administered rebaptism to adults, though the Zurich Council had expressly decreed that infant baptism must still remain the only valid form of baptism.

The other twenty-five were arrested because they had been baptized a second time in direct violation of the Council's decree of January 18. In reality, the number of those baptized in Zollikon up to that time was thirty-five. Therefore, only about two thirds of them were imprisoned on January 30.

Manz and Blaurock were put in the Zurich state prison, the Wellenberg tower which stood in the Limmat[1] (No. 37, 42d). This tower held only nine cells and so was too small to house the twenty-five Zollikon farmers. The Council therefore ordered that they be imprisoned in the Augustinian monastery in Zurich (No. 37). The monastery had been vacant only eight weeks, the monks having been forced to leave it on December 3, 1524. Now it was to serve as a prison for Anabaptists. The prisoners were lodged together in a hall of the monastery, probably the chapter hall or the refectory (No. 37).

The men from Zollikon were confined for nine days in the Augustinian cloister (January 30—February 8). They were being held for investigation. The prisoners were cross-examined. Beside the investigation, the second main purpose of the imprisonment was to reconvert the Anabaptists to the Zwinglian standpoint. One might call it a "conversion custody." A delegation was selected by the Council and appointed to go to the Anabaptists in the monastery and "listen and see in what they persist and what attitude they were taking" (No. 37).

The delegation consisted of the three city people's priests —Zwingli, Jud, and Megander—and of the three Council members who had supervised the arrest in Zollikon on January 30. That was a powerful concentration of forces. The representatives of government and of theology came to these country people in prison to dispute with them. In the face of this superior force the position of the prisoners was the more awkward, because they were separated from their spiritual leaders

44

(Brötli, Manz, and Blaurock) and were thrown entirely on their own resources.

The theological discussion in the Augustinian monastery concerned the Scriptural proof for rebaptism. Zwingli declared that nowhere in the Bible is there any mention of one and the same person being baptized twice. The men of Zollikon contradicted him by referring to Acts 19. Here in verses 1-7 it is recorded that Paul met some men in Ephesus who had been baptized by John the Baptist. "And Paul said, 'John baptized with the baptism of repentance, telling the people to believe in the one to come after him, that is Jesus.' On hearing this they were baptized in the name of the Lord Jesus."

These Ephesian disciples of John did in reality receive baptism twice, first from John the Baptist, then from Paul. Zwingli, however, would not admit this, the only possible interpretation. He maintained that these men were not baptized by John, but merely instructed by him. Only Paul had conferred water baptism on them (Nos. 43, 46).

This tortured interpretation was not convincing. We are therefore not astonished to hear that the prisoners felt themselves very sure in their cause. We have information about the feeling among them from Hans Hottinger.[2] He was a Zurich craftsman and served as night watchman on the side. He did not belong to the Anabaptists, but sympathized with them, and was also close kin to Conrad Hottinger of Zollikon, who was in the Augustinian jail. He was able to visit the prisoners without being seen, probably at night (Nos. 43, 46). Through him they sent a message to their relatives. And so after supper one evening of the first week in February, Hans Hottinger went to Zollikon. The families and friends of the arrested men were called together in the house of Hans Murer. There must have been a dozen men and few women present. To them Hans Hottinger related what he had heard and seen:

45

"Dear brethren, I am to greet you from the other brethren, and you must be fearless and of good courage, as they also are of good courage. They are getting along well." In answer to the question from the gathering concerning how the dispute over baptism between their "brothers in Christ" and Zwingli had developed, Hans Hottinger reported that Zwingli had thus far not been able to accomplish anything. "On the contrary," he added, "Your brothers have routed Zwingli!"

That sounds very boastful and doubtless does not correspond to the facts. Still it deals with a statement for which a reason is given, and we must examine the reason. The reference states, freely translated: "Hottinger answered: In regard to their discussion with Zwingli, it was possible for the brethren to convince Zwingli. For Zwingli declared to them, that when Lent comes he, too, would accept the godly life" (No. 43).

It is quite possible that Zwingli did say something similar. As we have already seen above, at that time (February, 1525) baptism and the Lord's Supper were still celebrated according to old Catholic usage in the city and its surrounding territory. It was the Anabaptists of Zollikon who no longer could endure this half measure and were the first to abolish the Roman rite. It is very probable that these questions came up for discussion in Zwingli's dispute in the Augustinian cloister. Zwingli may have declared that very soon, in Lent, he would carry through the reorganization of the ceremonies.

Actually he appeared before the Council on April 11 and demanded that the mass finally be abolished. The Council complied and abolished the celebration of the mass on April 12 (Wednesday after Palm Sunday). In its place came a liturgy of the Lord's Supper composed by Zwingli. At the same time a new ceremony for infant baptism was introduced which was disconnected from its Catholic origin.

In any case, Zwingli announced to his opponents in the

Augustinian cloister these reforms which were soon to take place, and perhaps he had also hoped in that way, at least in part, to take the wind out of the sails of the Anabaptist cause. The Anabaptists must have gained the impression that Zwingli was yielding to them on these liturgical points and interpreted it as a victory achieved over the Reformer.

According to the plausible story of night watchman Hans Hottinger, the attitude of the prisoners in the Augustinian monastery was unbroken. The report of their release, therefore, is unexpected. On February 7, the twenty-five men were sentenced to pay the cost of maintenance and a joint fine of one thousand gulden. On February 8, they were released on an oath of peace[3] (Nos. 37, 38). Manz and Blaurock, on the other hand, were still held in prison. The benefit of liberation could not be granted them since they were obstinate. And the twenty-five? They were not obstinate and could therefore be released.

Hans Hottinger's reports are therewith not refuted. When he visited the prisoners they were still very confident. But later came the hour when they yielded. They promised "that they would not do it any more." That meant they would recognize the infant baptism of the church and abstain from any further rebaptism in Zollikon. It meant, for them, giving up any Anabaptist church life.

That was a difficult decision. In order to lighten it somewhat the Council granted the twenty-five men of Zollikon a concession: They and their like-minded friends might still meet among themselves, but only in groups of three or four persons, and only for joint Bible reading and Bible discussion, but not for baptism and preaching (Nos. 76, 104, 106). Baptisms and sermons should remain the concern exclusively of the official pastors of Zollikon.

The report that the prisoners had yielded was sent to Brötli, who was staying in Hallau in the Canton of Schaffhausen. He dealt with it in a letter to the brothers in Zollikon. He was deeply troubled. His fears had come true. He reproved the prisoners for disowning the sign of baptism and letting their missionary activity be curtailed in a way which is clearly contrary to the Word of God.

Brötli had further learned that backsliding had also set in among the Zollikon Anabaptists who had not been imprisoned. Brötli saw the reason for their defection in their unwillingness to be loosed from earthly possessions. He pays a great tribute to Jörg Blaurock and Felix Manz who had not recanted, and remarks finally that besides himself, also Conrad Grebel, who was staying in Schaffhausen at that time, and Wilhelm Röubli are grieved over the Anabaptist church of Zollikon (No. 44).

IV

NEW IMPETUS

Brötli's unfavorable opinion seems to have been confirmed.
After the return of the prisoners from the Augustinian monastery everything was quiet in Zollikon so far as we can judge
from the sources. Then Blaurock appeared on the scene. This
fiery spirit fanned into new life the flame which had not been
extinguished but merely subdued to a glimmer.

On February 18 the Council had decided to release Blaurock upon an oath of peace (No. 42 e). A recantation was
not demanded of him. But before he left the jail he was to be
confronted with Zwingli and produce proof of the accusations
he had raised against him. The release, however, was not
made dependent on the outcome of this meeting. Blaurock
was to be turned loose. This magnanimous procedure stands
in sharp contrast to the decision which was at the same time
passed against Manz. Manz, who had not recanted any more
than Blaurock, was sentenced to further detention in the
Wellenberg Tower because of his stubbornness (No. 42 d).
Manz was a citizen of Zurich and had sworn allegiance to the
Zurich government. He was therefore treated more severely,
while Blaurock, a foreigner from the Grisons, was temporarily
more leniently dealt with.

Blaurock was set free on February 24. Where could he turn?
Of his friends in Zurich, Manz was in prison and Grebel was
no longer in Zurich territory. So he made his way to Heinrich
Aberli, one of the most faithful members of Grebel's circle;

Aberli was a baker on Rennweg in Zurich. For the reception of the released prisoner Aberli had invited three men to his house: tailor Hans Oggenfuss of Zurich, furrier Anton Roggenacher of Zurich, and winegrower Jacob Hottinger, one of the pillars of the group in Zollikon. Hottinger and Oggenfuss had been prisoners in the Augustinian monastery. The five ate supper together at Aberli's. "Then they spoke so much of God, that they at last desired the table of God, of which they partook with one another." So at their meal they engaged in religious talk, and the desire arose to experience the Lord's Supper without Catholic framing. Bread and wine were already at hand, since they were at supper. Then "God's table" was soon prepared, and the day was closed with a domestic Holy Supper (No. 50).

The only one who was aware of the revolutionary character of this private, solemn hour was Roggenacher. Aberli, Blaurock, Hottinger, and Oggenfuss had previously enjoyed fellowship with one another, but Roggenacher was a newcomer in this circle. He was frightened when he saw that his table companions were preparing to partake of the Lord's Supper, and asked them to pray God that he, too, might be inwardly prepared to take part. The other four fulfilled his request and prayed for him. And so Roggenacher, too, could participate in good conscience (No. 50).

Roggenacher must have been greatly impressed by Blaurock's personality and message. He saw him for the first time on the evening of February 24, and even before the meeting at Aberli's was over he asked him to come to his house in Stadelhofen the next day. This Blaurock did. He was the guest of Roggenacher from Saturday, February 25, to Sunday, February 26.

Blaurock felt that his host was open for repentance and conversion and told him that he must receive baptism as a sign

50

of the forgiveness of sins. Early Sunday morning he was ready and asked to be baptized. Blaurock gladly accommodated him, and so, adult baptism was administered to the furrier in Stadelhofen on the morning of February 26 (No. 50).

Such a prelude could not help but encourage a man like Blaurock to further action. It was the Sunday of "parsons' carnival,"[1] and in Zollikon everyone was resting from his labor. So Blaurock, accompanied by Aberli, Oggenfuss, and the Zurich goldsmith Hujuf, set out toward Zollikon.

In the forenoon, while the Reformed pastor Billeter was preaching in the Zollikon church, Blaurock held a revival meeting in the parlor of farmer Hans Murer in Gstad (today Bahnhofstrasse 3, Zollikon), and a second one after dinner (No. 48). This is the house where Brötli on January 27, 1525, had arranged the last baptismal gathering before his departure. Blaurock impressed upon his hearers their lostness in sin, with the result that after his second talk (afternoon) in Murer's house eight weeping women arose, went forward, and were baptized (with a dipper).

On the same day Blaurock also baptized Heinrich Aberli in the house of Jacob Hottinger (No. 54). The baptism of Aberli took place as follows: Blaurock asked: "Brother Heinrich, do you confess that the Lord Jesus Christ has suffered for us and that what is written about Him is true?" Aberli answered: "Yes." Thereupon Blaurock took a handful of water and sprinkled Aberli, with the words: "I baptize you in the name of the Father, and the Son, and the Holy Spirit." Thus baptism was performed in the name of the triune God, and prerequisite was the candidate's confession of redemption through Christ.

Of the eight women baptized we know the names of seven (No. 48): the wife of Lienhard Bleuler, the wife of Rutsch Hottinger, the wife of Jacob Unholz, the wife of Jörg Schad, the wife of Fridli Schumacher, Trini the daughter of Conrad Hottinger, and Urseli Frig of Balgrist (certainly the daughter of Heini Frig, called "Gigli"). The husbands of the first five women had been imprisoned in the Augustinian monastery, the fathers of Trini and Urseli likewise. These seven women and girls therefore came from Anabaptist families and did not signify a real new increase in the Zollikon church.

It might be assumed that the baptism of these women constituted a rather modest result of this Sunday's work and that this scarcely satisfied the apostolic urge of Blaurock. But perhaps he did not desire any more to begin with. After the difficult weeks which lay behind the young church, he was first of all concerned to strengthen its foundations. That could be achieved most naturally by also taking into the church the wives and grown daughters of the baptized men, so that the families would be welded into bearers of the free church idea. Only on this basis is the continuance of the church and its missionary work thinkable at all.

Besides, these women would certainly never have decided to be baptized if they had not had the support of their husbands and fathers, or even been induced to it by them. Lienhard Bleuler, Rutsch Hottinger, Jacob Unholz, Jörg Schad, Fridli Schumacher, Conrad Hottinger, and Heini Frig had, to be sure, promised to restrain themselves, but now they nevertheless became active again. How they could harmonize that with their promise we will have to ask later.

Blaurock remained in Zollikon only this one day, February 26. Then he moved on, but we do not know his destination. He never saw Zollikon again. The proximity of Zurich seems to have been too dangerous for him.

Again the brothers in Zollikon were thus thrown upon their own resources. At first after Blaurock's departure quiet reigned for ten days, at least outwardly. But then the turns. On Wednesday, March 8, the Lord's Supper is observed by the lake in the orchard of Hans Murer, that is, in the open (No. 56). On the following Sunday, March 12, farmer Jörg Schad baptized about forty persons, and surprisingly this occurred in the Zollikon church (Nos. 55, 104, 105). From March 8 to March 15 about thirty additional people were baptized by Hans Bichter, a man from the Black Forest who was employed as a tailor apprentice by Hans Rey in Zollikon (No. 56). Oggenfuss baptized the younger Jacob Hottinger, Valentin Gredig baptized a woman, Hujuf baptized two men (No. 56), and Jacob Hottinger the younger baptized seven persons.

A communion service in the open in broad daylight, a rebaptism in the church on Sunday—these show that the Anabaptist farmers in Zollikon had lost all reticence. They took the leadership of their fellowship into their own hands. They held meetings embracing more than the allowed four persons, in which they not only read the Bible but also preached (No. 57).

Five places of meeting are mentioned: the homes of Jacob Hottinger, Uli Hottinger, Hans Murer, Heini Murer, and a man by the name of Ruh who is not referred to elsewhere (No. 104). They baptized (No. 57). In every assembly they celebrated the Lord's Supper (No. 56). This is the "priesthood of all believers" which the New Testament and the Reformation proclaimed as the ideal. Increasingly the group in Zollikon had become shepherdless. Brötli and Blaurock had departed and Felix Manz was imprisoned. Now they summoned courage to make use of the right of the lay priesthood.

These events did not take place without order. A kind of church organization seems to have existed. Besides the baptizing brothers—mainly Schad, Bichter, and the younger Hottinger—there were preachers and readers—especially Rutsch Hottinger and old Jacob Hottinger— (Nos. 56, 57). Old Jacob

Hottinger may have been considered as the head of the fellowship. He was also the one who introduced church discipline in the congregation (No. 58). Anyone who offended against the duties laid upon the baptized members was excluded. This regulation, incidentally, weakens the view that those Anabaptists considered themselves as sinless. They knew that sins occurred in their ranks, and therefore they established a procedure, in accordance with Matthew 18:15-20, for disciplining the sinful brother.

Since the brotherhood of Zollikon practiced preaching, baptism, the Lord's Supper, and church discipline, it possessed the four characteristics of an independent Christian church.

In the week of March 8-15 at least eighty persons were baptized in Zollikon. That appears to be a great increase in the Zollikon Anabaptist congregation. But of these eighty, only about one fourth hailed from Zollikon; and the majority of these were women, among whom we meet even the wife of deputy bailiff Hans Wüest, president of the village of Zollikon.

The other sixty nearly all came from Höngg and Küsnacht (No. 55). Küsnacht was the neighboring village to Zollikon and had been infected from there. The village of Höngg was located somewhat farther away, but had been spiritually prepared for the Anabaptist movement by its former pastor Simon Stumpf. In Zollikon itself the ability to absorb the message of the Anabaptists was at that time practically exhausted. The movement therefore now spread beyond the previous limits and entered new territories.

This is probably the proper moment to recall the words which Brötli had written to the Zollikon brothers after the prisoners had returned from the Augustinian monastery. The prisoners had promised to desist from further activity. Hence Brötli accused them of recanting, and we sense from his lines that he had really given up faith in any renewal of the Zollikon church. Brötli's gloomy prediction had not yet come true; his censure was premature. He was probably satisfied with the unexpected turn of events in Zollikon, although we have no report to that effect.

V

RENEWED IMPRISONMENT

The ill humor was now to be found on the part of the authorities. They must have felt themselves deceived by the men of Zollikon, at least by those who had been imprisoned in the monastery. Of the twenty-five men who on February 8 had promised to keep still, twenty-two had participated in the renewal of the church during the five weeks since their release. Only three had remained quite passive. The rest had broken their promise.

They were therefore brought before the judge for questioning. Rutsch Hottinger, one of the leaders in the Zollikon circle, gives the following answer: "What we promised in the Augustinian prison, namely, that we would stand still, we have kept. We stood still until God bade us to do otherwise" (No. 54).

Thus the assurance which the brothers had given the Council on February 8 was subject to an unspoken reservation: They would remain still provided God himself did not call them to action. This call had come, probably on the Sunday[1] of "parsons' carnival," as Blaurock appeared in their midst. And God's command, of course, stood above the command of men. Whether the twenty-five had agreed among themselves while still in jail to consider their assurance as only conditional, or if they interpreted it so later, perhaps under Blaurock's influence, can no longer be ascertained.

The authorities, as was to be expected, showed no understanding for this mental reservation. Moreover, on March 16,

1525, they arrested all who had baptized in Zollikon (No. 53). The following were taken into custody: Heinrich Aberli, Konrad Baumann, Lienhard Bleuler, Rudolf Breitiner, Hans Bichter, Gabriel Giger, Valentin Gredig, Heini Hottinger, Jacob Hottinger the younger, Hans Hottinger the watchman, Rutsch Hottinger, Philipp Kym, Hans Murer, Klaus Murer, Hans Oggenfuss, Anton Roggenacher, Michael Sattler, Jörg Schad, and Fridli Schumacher (Nos. 54-64), a total of nineteen men. Four of these nineteen had practiced rebaptism in the last weeks, and in reality the arrest order concerned only these four. But since it was not immediately known who they were, all those who were suspected of baptizing were taken into custody. This list therefore includes nearly all the responsible Anabaptist personalities in Zollikon and Zurich at that time.

After March 16, therefore, the Anabaptists constituting the leadership in Zollikon and Zurich were in prison. Again they were being held for questioning. They remained until March 25, nine days, just as in the case of the first imprisonment (January 30—February 8). The procedure during this second nine-day period was similar to that of the first nine days.

The prisoners were examined by Councilors appointed for the task. The questions were (No. 59): What have you been doing since February 8? Have you been reading (that is, have you conducted Bible studies)? Have you baptized? Have you seen anyone baptize? Have you been baptized? For what reason did you let yourself be baptized? This last question all of them answered in the same way: The Holy Scriptures have led us to baptism (Nos. 54, 60). Gredig, the farmhand from Safien in the Grisons, who was employed by Ruedi Thomann, cited Mark 16:16 and Matthew 28:19 ("He who believes and is baptized will be saved" and "make disciples . . . baptizing them").

57

These Anabaptists were not spiritualists who depended on personal illumination, but they were Biblicists, who found their guidance in the Bible and the fullest possible compliance with it. By so clearly stating, one after the other, that they had been instructed concerning baptism by the Word of God, they were trying to exclude the idea that they had been guided or even led astray by human teachers. These men from Zollikon and Zurich wanted to be considered responsible Christians and Bible readers.

As soon as the accused took recourse to the Bible, the Councilors were no longer competent. What were they to do now? They could have insisted on the binding government decree and declared: For us the Zwinglian concept of baptism is authoritative, and you must bow to it. But this they did not say. They did not want to change minds by force, but hoped that the turn might be accomplished by inner conviction.

The last question put to the prisoners by the Councilors was therefore phrased (No. 54): Are you willing to be corrected by the Holy Scriptures? Most of them declared that in principle they were willing to do so, and now the representatives of the Council transferred their task to the theologians.

Zwingli appeared personally in the prison to conduct the discussion (No. 64). This time he had better success than five weeks before, when the Anabaptists proclaimed that they had changed Zwingli's mind. Zwingli now had more power to achieve his ends because several factors came to his aid. Upon the order of the Council the Anabaptists had again been put in the Augustinian monastery; this time, however, not in one hall, but each in a separate cell (No. 49). This was obviously a deliberate attempt to "divide and conquer." This measure was intended to weaken their group spirit. Consider the fact that Zwingli and the Council members disputed with the simple farmers and craftsmen one by one in their cells. It required steel nerves to meet such a situation.

A second factor aiding Zwingli's instruction was the threat hanging over the prisoners. They were released on March 25, with the announcement that a relapse would bring banishment (No. 65). This had of course already been announced to them before their release and had without question influenced the outcome of the Zwinglian instruction. Most of them declared that they were ready to accept Zwingli's views. Certainly not all of them did so on the basis of pure conviction. The pressure, however, was too great.

Thus the outcome of the second imprisonment in the Augustinian monastery is not a surprise. On March 25, only four of the nineteen Anabaptists stood by their confession: Jörg Schad, Gabriel Giger, Rutsch Hottinger, and Jacob Hottinger, the younger (No. 64). The other fifteen promised that "they would desist from such rebaptism and neither speak nor act against infant baptism."

So the second round was lost. This time there followed no new upswing, but only a revolt by a few leading men and an outburst of wrath by the people.

VI

THE PROPHETS OF ZOLLIKON

In June, 1525, a peculiar procession wends its way toward Zurich—men, women, and children wearing willow twigs or ropes instead of belts. They are men and women from the farms of Zollikon. They proceed through the lanes and squares of Zurich, doubtless an astounding sight to the citizens of the town. Quite unheard-of is the message they bring.

With loud voices these Zollikon people brand the Reformer Zwingli as the dragon of whom John's Revelation had prophesied (Revelation 12:3). They call the inhabitants of Zurich to repentance and threaten that "if you do not repent, a dreadful calamity will befall you!" Thus God's doom is announced to impenitent Zurich. And this announcement is underscored through cries of woe. Zwingli, to whom we are indebted for our knowledge of this procession, relates what he heard: "On the streets they cried horribly: Woe, Woe! Woe to Zurich! Some of them, following Jonah's example, gave the city forty days of grace."[1]

In the history of Zurich there is only one event somewhat similar to this procession, namely the "Zurich putsch" of September 6, 1839, when Bible-believing country people thronged to Zurich to force the dismissal of David Friedrich Strauss, a professor of theology who was critical of the Bible.

In both instances a religiously rooted indignation in the country is directed against the city. But the events in 1525 are more amazing than the happening in 1839. For in 1839 the

60

country people enjoyed the same rights as the city population, whereas in 1525 the country was completely subject to the rule of the city. Under these circumstances it was very difficult, indeed dangerous, in the sixteenth century for the country to criticize the city, while in the nineteenth century it had become easy. The inner "shock" required in 1525 for small farmers to leave their villages to admonish the conscience of the all-powerful city was greater than that needed for the "Zurich putsch." The question arises concerning where the people of Zollikon got the courage for this venture.

They felt themselves to be the messengers of God, commissioned with the message of repentance and judgment. We call such people prophets. The prophets in the Bible, from Amos to Jesus Christ, called for repentance. If the people repented they would find salvation, if they did not repent they would perish. We read in Isaiah 33:15 ff. that he who walks in righteousness and refuses to take a bribe will escape judgment. That is the prophetic promise of salvation. But if the call goes unheeded and hearts harden, then a Jeremiah calls out his "Woe unto thee, O Jerusalem" (Jeremiah 13:27)! And Jesus His: "Woe unto thee, Chorazin! woe unto thee, Bethsaida" (Matthew 11:21)! Thus the prophecy of salvation turns to the prophecy of doom. This same rhythm we also find in the attitude of the prophets of Zollikon.

It is evident that in their procession calling for repentance they have been influenced by the example of the Biblical prophets. This becomes particularly patent on two points. First, in their imitation of the prophet Jonah. Just as he went to the city of Nineveh and preached: "Yet forty days, and Nineveh shall be overthrown" (Jonah 3:4), so they went to the city of Zurich and proclaimed its destruction in forty days. Secondly, they have changed part of their clothing under the influence of another verse in the Prophets. Isaiah says that when the judgment of God comes, they shall wear "instead of a girdle, a rope" (Isaiah 3:24). It was certainly on the basis of this verse that some of the prophets of Zollikon laid aside their belts and substituted a rope. They wanted by this symbolic act to underscore the seriousness of the hour.

Others had tied willow twigs around them instead of belts. Where this notion comes from, I was not able to trace. Perhaps it is to be understood as a symbolic representation of the rod of divine chastisement: "Then will I visit their transgression with the rod" (Psalm 89:32).

Reference should be made to still another feature in which the prophets of Zollikon evidently deviated from the Biblical pattern. The great prophets delivered the message committed to them individually and often as lonely men. But the prophets of Zollikon appeared jointly in Zurich, and even women and children participated. It may at first seem as if there is no Biblical precedent for such a troop of prophets and prophetesses. We may, however, recall that the prophet Joel predicted, in the well-known statement, that the time would come when God will pour out His Spirit upon all flesh, and their sons and their daughters shall prophesy (Joel 2:28). It is possible that it was this promise which generated the collective prophesying of the men and women of Zollikon.

In regard to the identification of Zwingli with the dragon we must look at the context in which the Biblical reference to the dragon occurs. The dragon in Revelation persecutes the woman, that is, the Christian church (Revelation 12:4). The young Anabaptist church regarded itself as the true church and found itself attacked by Zwingli. So its members could easily be led to find their lot predicted in Revelation 12. Since the persecution of the Christians by the dragon takes place in the last days, it follows that the Anabaptists of Zollikon considered the Judgment Day to be at hand.

The prophetic procession in Zurich in 1525 was not the only undertaking of this kind. We know similar incidents from later Anabaptist history. On February 8, 1534, before the establishment of the Anabaptist kingdom of Münster in Westphalia (Germany), the Anabaptist prophets Knipperdolling and Bockelson ran through the city and cried, as eyewitness Kerssenbroich reports: "Woe, woe, woe to you who laugh to scorn us who are driven by the divine Spirit, you who do not give heed to the voice proclaiming saving repentance, you who despise our covenant; repent and turn lest you draw upon yourselves the punishment of the heavenly Father."

Three days later a flock of Anabaptist women proceeded through the streets of the same city. "You ungodly people," they said, "why do you persist so long in your filthy ungodliness? Now is the time of repentance! The axe has already been laid at the root of the trees. Repent, repent! Do you not yet discern that the Father is wroth with you and that perdition and total destruction await you?" In February, 1535, seven men and five women ran naked through the streets of Amsterdam and cried: "Woe, woe, woe!"

We know that the source of this cry of penance and woe lies in the ideas of Melchior Hofmann, of Schwäbisch-Hall. The prophets of Münster and Amsterdam were Melchiorites. Hofmann had figured out on the basis of Daniel and Revelation that the last day was close at hand and had thereby awakened in certain Anabaptist groups a "last-days" attitude which kept intensifying until it came to a terrible eruption in the "kingdom of God" at Münster.

As simple as it is to discover the spiritual origin of the Münster and Amsterdam prophets, it is just as difficult to show in detail how the prophesying of judgment over Zurich by the Anabaptists of Zollikon arose. Melchior Hofmann had no connection with Zollikon. Furthermore, there is no evidence that he occupied himself with the return of Christ before the summer of 1525. One might assume that even before Hofmann came up with his eschatological reflections in Germany, the Anabaptists in Zollikon also expected the imminent end of the world, and on the basis of the Prophets and Apocalypse meditated on the coming kingdom of God.

But it is certainly not an everyday occurrence for simple village people and subjects to band themselves together and march to the neighboring capital in order to fling against it prophecies of doom in a spirit of prophetic self-assurance. The souls of these people must surely have been literally satiated with apocalyptic and prophetic pictures.

Yet for this assumption we cannot really produce any documentary proof. In the court records of the hearing already mentioned such a fixation on the last days does not appear at all. But, in addition to these documents of 1524 and 1525, about two dozen letters have been preserved which were written by the Anabaptists belonging to the Zurich and Zollikon circles. Only in two of them—two letters by Conrad Grebel (Nos. 16, 63)—is an eschatological note discernible, but only as something incidental. All the other writings deal with right preaching, true to the Bible, the building up of the true church, baptism, defense against false accusations, and perseverance. The Prophets and the Apocalypse are not cited anywhere except in the two letters by Grebel.

The expectation of the end of the world by these Anabaptists does not seem to have differed from the usual one in that period. We do notice, of course, that a wave of deep revival, accompanied by strong emotional expression, passed through Zollikon early in 1525, but this excitement revolved about the poles of sin and forgiveness, not about the end of the world.

All the more astonishing is this prophetic procession. It seems to have been unprepared. Like a great boulder thrown out of a volcano it is suddenly there. We can only record that it did happen, but we cannot illuminate the inner process of its formation. We sense that under the cover of the faith of the Zollikon Anabaptists, known to us from documents and letters, there also lay hidden a prophetic-eschatological undercurrent. This flow, brought forth out of the hidden depths, so that it temporarily came to light and formed itself into a procession calling for repentance, may have had its source in the inner condition of the Zollikon Anabaptist movement in June, 1525. The backbone of the church was broken. Dissolution was her destiny. The result was a great disappointment with the city of Zurich and with its spiritual head, Huldrych Zwingli. Many Zollikon Anabaptists in that moment of despair were convinced in earnest that the city deserved divine condemnation, and could be saved only by speedy conversion.

It is also possible that a certain personality had started the stone rolling in that month of June, namely Hans Hottinger of Zollikon. On the Sunday of Pentecost, June 4, 1525, he disturbed the sermon of Pastor Billeter in the church of Zollikon by turning to the congregation and crying: "Go out, go out and protect yourselves from the false prophet" (that is, from the pastor) (No. 73). This outcry began with the explosion of an individual, but it was also surely the sign of a ferment, or rather a fever, which at that time had gripped many members of the hard-pressed church in Zollikon. Hottinger may have given the signal for the prophetic march on Zurich.

The cry of woe in Zurich in 1525 is not characteristic of the piety of the early Anabaptists; it is an exception. But it does indicate what tremendous inner energies the Anabaptist movement produced—energies which could also become destructive when misused by infamous men (Münster!).

VII

FINAL DISSOLUTION

It would, however, be one-sided to see the end of the Anabaptist movement in Zollikon only in the light of the prophetic procession. For it is most striking that this odd incident is not mentioned in the contemporary documents of the court hearings. For the year 1525 there are some forty official court records of statements made by the Anabaptists who were imprisoned in Zurich. Nowhere in these testimonies do we find even a reference to the event about which Zwingli speaks. That is explained by the fact that the Zurich Council did not take legal action against the participants in this woe-procession. No arrests were made in connection with it, and therefore no entry was made concerning it in the records.

But why did not the officials institute a lawsuit against the participants and the inciters of the procession? Did the Council at that time (June, 1525) perhaps regard the problem in Zollikon as already solved, so that it would serve no purpose to deal with it again? That is not the case. Zollikon remained as before, a storm center which had to be closely watched by the Zurich government. This is shown by the wave of arrests in August, 1525. In that month the leading personalities of the Zollikon brotherhood were imprisoned anew, and most of them, as it soon turned out, under false suspicion, so that they were quickly released. This precipitate arrest shows how anxiously the Zurich authorities kept an eye on the Anabaptists of Zollikon.

And yet no prosecution for the procession! Evidently the

members of the Council considered it as a single lapse by enthusiasts and knew that the responsible Anabaptists of Zollikon did not participate in it. This I conclude from the fact that not one of the men arrested in Zollikon in 1525 was questioned about this procession during the hearings.

The core of the Zollikon church did not consist of enthusiasts. Let us again raise the question about the lot of this sound core. At the end of March, 1525, the leading members of the fellowship were punished and then given their freedom. A continuance of the separatist Anabaptist church was strictly forbidden.

In July, 1525, there came an appeal to the Zollikon Christian brothers from the hamlet of Wassberg (Maur commune in the canton of Zurich) and from the Nänikon commune (canton of Zurich) for men who could read to them from the Bible. The brothers decided to send Rudolf Rutschmann, Rutsch Hottinger, and Felix Kienast to Wassberg and Nänikon (No. 76).

From this we see that the brotherhood is still together. It has not been dissolved. It does not sit in idleness, but wants to contribute what it can toward satisfying the hunger for the Bible; and therefore, when asked, it sends into the surrounding villages farmers who can read.

The three Bible readers were arrested and asked how they could reconcile their activity with the prohibition of the Anabaptist church. Rudolf Rutschmann reminded them in his answer that the Councilors had once permitted the Zollikon brothers "to go to each other to read, and also to instruct each other and teach the Word of God." He added, "We have done nothing else than this in Zollikon. And as the request came to our church from the outside, our church went outside also only as readers, not as baptizing messengers" (No. 76).

The permission to hold private gatherings had been granted

to the Anabaptists on February 7, 1525, at the same time when they were prohibited from maintaining a separate church. They were not to baptize any more, but among themselves they might meet for Bible study. The friends in Zollikon did at that time, as we have seen, make use of this opportunity until Blaurock came and the baptizing started again.

On March 25 followed a new prohibition against baptizing, that is, against founding their own church. The suppressed group now reflected on the permission granted on February 7, and again built Bible circles in Zollikon, expecting in this way to salvage what they could. At the same time they carried on a "reduced program."

The Zurich Council had intended such gatherings to take place within the church; that is, the participants in these Bible groups should also go to church and regard themselves as members of the state church. In this hope they were disappointed.

The brothers of Zollikon limited themselves to their own Bible groups and ignored the church services and the pastor. This development the Council could not permit. It therefore forbade private gatherings. In August, 1525, Jacob Hottinger, the leader of the Zollikon circle, received a writ from the city hall in Zurich decreeing that "he, this Hottinger and others, should not gang together, but go to church and there hear the word of God" (No. 101).

With that the Zollikon brothers were forced to a clear decision. In that very month they met to counsel about what they were to do now (No. 105). The place of their conference was the home of Heini Hottinger. The number of those present was thirty. We recall that the number arrested in the Augustinian cloister in January, 1525, was also about thirty men. Now we meet the same number in August, and that indicates that the leading circle in the Zollikon Anabaptist movement had remained about the same.

The thirty companions in the Hottinger home arrived at the decision "to give up baptizing, simply live the Christian life together, and be obedient to my lords" (No. 105). This is to be understood as follows: The plan to organize an Anabaptist free church in Zollikon was buried; also the gatherings in the houses here and there were discontinued; the brothers would still remain bound to each other in the Christian spirit, but without an independent organization; they would render obedience to the regulations of the Council in regard to church attendance and membership in the state church.

With this decision the brothers of Zollikon made their peace with the state and with the church. It was a peace caused by fatigue. The various restrictions and punishments had in eight months undermined their resistance.

In the spring of 1526, brothers Heini and Uli Hottinger again dared to raise the issue by casting doubt on the validity of infant baptism (No. 170 b, 173). When they were arrested, they quickly gave in.

In June, 1527, a group of five former Zollikon Anabaptists reappear in the court documents (No. 219). Jacob Falk and Heini Reimann, two farmers from the upper territory of Zurich, were at that time jailed in the Governor's Castle at Grüningen, and it was expected that they would be sentenced to death because of rebaptizing. This was done in 1528. In order to comfort the prisoners, Jacob, Uli, and Heini Hottinger, along with Jacob Unholz and Felix Kienast, traveled to Grüningen (June, 1527) and there obtained permission to speak with Falk and Reimann. The Zollikon men encouraged their deathmarked friends and exhorted them to remain faithful to the truth to the end. Uli Hottinger confessed that he had given the imprisoned brothers his hand, had encouraged them, and said that they should be steadfast and brave and not recant.

What astounds us in this exhortation is that it comes from the mouths of men who had themselves recanted. For all five visitors had denied their own faith and had not found strength for martyrdom. And yet they could bring themselves to call on others to be steadfast. In any event, Unholz, Kienast, and the three Hottingers felt themselves united in a common faith with the two imprisoned Anabaptists, and thereby revealed, if it still needs proof, that the Anabaptists of Zollikon had returned to the state church only because of despondency and fear, and not from conviction.

After June, 1527, the waves in Zollikon subside (outwardly). The disturbers are finally checkmated (Jacob Hottinger excepted). Three formerly influential persons in the Anabaptist church fell as Zurich warriors in the Battle of Kappel in October, 1531 (Heini Hottinger, Felix Kienast, and Hans Murer). They lay on the battlefield along with Zwingli and pastor Jacob Billeter of Zollikon, both of whom also met a soldier's death at Kappel. Thus death united those whom life had separated.

The staunchest among the Anabaptist insurgents of Zollikon was the farmer Jacob Hottinger the elder, whom we earlier designated as the spiritual leader of the church. He was imprisoned for the third time in August, 1526, because he had again let himself be carried away to criticize infant baptism (No. 187). He yielded and was released. In June, 1527, he was among those who encouraged the incarcerated Anabaptists in Grüningen. In April, 1528, we find him in jail again because he had arranged meetings and stayed away from church services (No. 254).

What induced Jacob Hottinger to this insubordinate attitude was not separatism and crankiness. Rather, before his eyes stood in particular brilliance the picture of what the early Anabaptist movement had sought to achieve. A great, new idea had made him a fighter and, in the end, a man who walked alone. It was the idea of personal religious freedom and the free church. This finds expression in the answer he gave his judges in August, 1525, in clumsy language, but unmistakably clear in meaning (No. 101).

Jacob Hottinger was opposed to the institution of a state church, "for it is not given to any government to dispose over God's Word with worldly means of force; is not after all the word of God free?" Assent to God's Word cannot be commanded, and therefore the state is not to concern itself at all with matters of faith. Taking his stand on this insight, Hottinger begged the Council members not to compel him to attend church, but to allow him to exercise his faith outside the state-led church. Thus he demanded toleration also for those who do not recognize the prevailing church form. He demanded the human right of individual liberty of conscience and of voluntary formation of the church.

This request by Jacob Hottinger, springing from the primitive Christian and reformational fountainhead, constituted the fulcrum and the core of the whole Anabaptist movement. And the village of Zollikon on Lake Zurich was the place where, within Protestant history, the first attempt was made to bring into being a Christian community independent of the state and resting on voluntary membership.

Such an experiment was bound to fail in its first attempt, and the only "mistake" of which we may accuse the men and women of Zollikon would be that they went at their task too early, before the time was ripe. In reality, that was no fault but an heroic deed. There will always be a need for men who, unconfused by the spirit of the age, set out for new goals and strive toward a new dawn. The Zollikon "Brothers in Christ" were such a vanguard. Their daring has not been in vain. In gratitude we bow before them today.

1 Translator's note: The word "Anabaptist" is used in this book to translate the German word "Taufer," which literally means "baptizer." "Anabaptist" literally means "re-baptizer" and corresponds strictly to the German word "Wiedertäufer," a word which in German usually has a connotation of scorn. "Täufer" could of course be translated by the word "baptist" (cf. John the Baptist); but the capitalized word has today become a technical term for historically more recent denominations. "Anabaptist" has, on the other hand, become the accepted term by church historians for the various "Täufer" movements which form such a dramatic part of the Reformation. It seems best to employ the term according to its accepted usage rather than its etymology. "Täufergemeinde" is therefore rendered "Anabaptist church," "Täufertum" is translated "Anabaptist movement."

2 The City Council of Zurich had jurisdiction also over the adjoining territory (see page 69).

3 The numbers refer to volume, page, and line of the critical Zwingli edition: Huldrych Zwingli's Sämtliche Werke, edited by Egli, et al., Zurich, 1952.

4 The cathedral of Zurich.

5 Harold S. Bender: Conrad Grebel, published in Goshen, Indiana, 1950, p. 101.

6 Printed as No. 8 in Quellen zur Geschichte der Täufer in der Schweiz, Vol. I, edited by Leonhard von Muralt and Walter Schmid and published in Zurich in 1952.

7 Critical Zwingli edition VI, 34,1-40,4.

8 Printed as No. 14 in Quellen zur Geschichte der Täufer in der Schweiz by Muralt and Schmid. The numbers above and in the following pages refer to pages and lines in this source collection.

9 Critical Zwingli edition, VI, 36-40.

10 Muralt and Schmid, op. cit., p. 24, lines 5-6.

11 Printed as No. 16 by Muralt and Schmid, op. cit.

12 Printed in the critical Zwingli edition, Vol. III, pp. 374-469.

13 Muralt and Schmid, op. cit., No. 22.

14 Also called Reublin in Anabaptist literature.

FOOTNOTES, PART 2

1 The numbers in this and the following chapters refer to Muralt and Schmid, op. cit.

2 In eastern Switzerland.

3 The Reformation and the Older Reform Parties.

4 "Perditi homines mediocrium bona communia volunt esse, sua vero, si quae habent, mullatenus," Elenchus in catabaptistarum strophas, 1527.

5 Critical Zwingli edition, VI, pp. 83-85.

6 *Das alte Zollikon* (1899).

7 *Die Bevälkerung Zollikons im Mittelalter und in der Neuzeit* (1946).

8 *"terrores conscientiae."*

FOOTNOTES, PART 3

1 The river flowing from Lake Zurich through the city of Zurich.

2 Not identical with the Anabaptist Hans Hottinger named on page 45.

3 "Urfehde," a legally binding oath to keep the peace.

FOOTNOTE, PART 4

1 *Pfaffenfastnacht*, literally "the eve before parsons' fasting," was observed by the clergy seven weeks before Easter (in 1525 Easter Sunday came on April 16). The usual Lent starts with Ash Wednesday forty days before Easter.

FOOTNOTE, PART 5

1 February 26, 1525.

FOOTNOTE, PART 6

1 Critical Zwingli edition VI, p. 43.

NOTES

The title *Brüder in Christo* (*Brothers in Christ*) is used for the Swiss edition of this book. This is what the Anabaptists of Zollikon called themselves; e.g., in No. 48 of the work: *Quellen zur Geschichte der Täufer in der Schweiz*, Volume I, edited by Leonhard von Muralt and Walter Schmid, Zurich, 1952.

Page 7: The exact title of the "Critical Zwingli edition" is: *Huldrych Zwingli's Sämtliche Werke,* edited by Emil Egli, Georg Finsler, Walther Köhler, Oskar Farner, Leonhard von Muralt, and Fritz Blanke (so far 10 volumes have appeared).

Page 8: Details of Grebel's life are found in Harold S. Bender's book: *Conrad Grebel,* published in Goshen, Indiana, 1950; and of the life of Manz in the scholarly biography by Ekkehard Krajewski, *Leben und Sterben des Zürcher Täuferführers Felix Mantz,* published by J. G. Oncken Verlag, Kassel, Germany, 1957.

Page 10: Bender's view (*Conrad Grebel,* p. 99) that Grebel and Stumpf as early as the Second Disputation had practically rejected the state church and had sponsored the idea of a free church, seems to me to be questionable.

Page 11: In *De canone missae epichiresis,* August, 1523, Zwingli expressly approves the wearing of chasubles and the use of the Latin language in the celebration of the Lord's Supper (Critical Zwingli edition, Vol. II, p. 660 ff.). A really new evangelical liturgy for the Lord's Supper was not established in Zurich until Easter, 1525 (Critical Zwingli edition, Vol. IV, pp. 1-24).

Page 12: "Iam ecclesiam piorum suis, iisque piis, senatum suum lecturam esse votis. Palam enim esse, quam multi sint et in senatu et in hac promiscua ecclesia impii" (Critical Zwingli edition, Vol. VI, 33,13-34,1). *Senatus* here means the secular Council, which is clearly distinguished from the *ecclesia.* We should not therefore, as Bender (*Grebel,* p. 255) correctly remarks, in this place understand by *senatus* a church authority, such as a synod. "The ecclesia of the pious will according to the wishes of their own pious (members) choose their own Council." That means: The believing Christians will, when they have the majority, carry through the election of the new Council in Zurich in the guilds. At that time in Zurich the Council was always chosen by the guilds, and not directly by the people.

Page 13: Grebel writes that he had read two of Müntzer's writings: *Von dem getichten Glauben* and *Protestation oder Empietung* (13,22). The main content of these two writings is Müntzer's mysticism of the cross which he drew from the Middle Ages. Grebel did not recognize nor understand this fundamentally mystical attitude of Müntzer. He takes over, in part to be sure, Müntzer's mystical conceptions, but gives them a Biblical meaning (13,32-33; 16,31; 17,28-29). A new proof of the Biblicism of the oldest Anabaptist movement.

74

Page 14: Cf. also 15, 2: Everything which is not specifically taught in the Bible should be abolished.

Page 15: "Sy gebruchend ouch weder weltlichs schwert noch krieg" (17,31). By "weltlichs schwert" is meant the office of government (according to Romans 13:4).

Page 17: Under the influence of Wilhelm Röubli, pastor in Witikon, near Zurich, the farmers Hans Huber and Rudolf Maler in Witikon refused already in March, 1524, to bring their newborn infants to baptism (No. 11). Under Brötli's influence three farmers in Zollikon followed their example in the summer of 1524 (also No. 11).

Page 18: The writing *Wer Ursache gebe zu Aufruhr* is also printed in the original text in *Zwingli, Hauptschriften,* edited by F. Blanke, O. Farner, R. Pfister, Vol. 7, pp. 127-228, published by the Zwingliverlag, Zurich, 1942.

Page 20: Fritz Blanke, "Ort und Zeit der ersten Wiedertaufe," *Theologische Zeitschrift,* 1952, pp. 74-76.

Page 22: For information about Fridli Schumacher see the statement by Heinrich Bruppacher on page 74 of the book by Heinrich Bruppacher and Alexander Nüesch, *Das alte Zollikon,* 1899.

Page 22: In Nos. 29 and 31 of *Quellen zur Geschichte der Täufer in der Schweiz* by L. von Muralt and W. Schmid, Brötli is called "the old helper," that is, the former helper (pastor). Brötli had been pastor in Quarten by Walensee, Switzerland, before he moved to Zollikon.

Page 24: The baptismal liturgy by Leo Jud, which was introduced in Zurich in 1523, still contained all these Catholic features (Critical Zwingli edition, Vol. IV, pp. 710-713). Not until the spring of 1525 did Zurich accept a really evangelical baptismal service composed by Zwingli (*op. cit.* Vol. IV, pp. 334-336).

Page 24: The data about this earliest Lord's Supper are not quite certain. It is clear that Grebel observed this Supper after he had had himself baptized, that is, after January 21, 1525. When Oggenfuss was questioned by the court he stated that this Lord's Supper had taken place fourteen days before. He was questioned as a witness between January 30 and February 7. If we count fourteen days back from February 7, we come to January 25. Grebel must have administered the Lord's Supper between Sunday, January 22 and January 25, probably early in that week. Bender also assumes in his book *Conrad Grebel* (1950), p. 138, that the Lord's Supper concerning which Oggenfuss testified was the *first* celebrated in the new Anabaptist church.

Page 24: Monstrance in the Reformed church: see No. 29 and also the Critical Zwingli edition, Vol. IV, p. 4.

Page 30: Gatherings in the evening: Hans Thomann testified that he had seen people with torches come and go to the meetings (No. 29).

Page 31: About Blaurock, see Oskar Vasella, "Von den Anfängen der bündnerischen Täuferbewegung," *Zeitschrift für Schweizerische Geschichte* (1939), p. 165 f.; and John Allen Moore, *Der starke Jörg*, J. G. Oncken Verlag, Kassel, Germany, 1955.

Page 31: First appearance of Blaurock in Zurich: *Geschicht-Buch der Hutterischen Brüder,* p. 34, edited by Rudolf Wolkan. The "Gespräch von Glaubenshändeln" referred to here may have been the discussion of baptism in Zurich, January 17, 1525.

Page 39: See Gottfried Wilhelm Locher, *Christus unser Hauptmann,* Zwingliana 1950, Heft 1.

Page 40: Zwingli against interference by the government in religious questions: In his pamphlet, *Adversus Hieronymum Emserum Antibolon,* bearing the date August 20, 1524, Zwingli emphasizes strongly the rights of the individual churches. They alone may judge the pastors and their teaching and excommunicate the impenitent; in Corinth every individual was permitted to speak in the worship service (I Cor. 14:29-32), and so it should be today also (Critical Zwingli edition, Vol. III, p. 261 f.).

Page 46: Social position of the Anabaptists in Zollikon: see the substantial investigation by Paul Peachey, *Die soziale Herkunft der Schweizer Täufer der Reformationszeit,* 1954.

Page 41: Reformational origin of the Zollikon Anabaptists: The thesis propounded by Alexander Rempel at the Mennonite Historical Conference in Göttingen, 1955, that the Zurich Anabaptists had been decisively influenced in their initial stages by the "Bohemian Brethren," I hold to be quite untenable. Had this dependency been reality, Zwingli would surely have known about it and spoken of it in his fight against the Anabaptists. But he says explicitly (in connection with I John 2:19): "They (the Anabaptists) went out from us, but they were not of us" (Critical Zwingli edition, Vol. VI, p. 47). It is also significant that in Grebel's letters to Müntzer (September, 1524), in which Grebel expresses himself very openly about the beginning of the Anabaptist movement in Zurich, there is no reference to a Bohemian influence.

Page 45: Referring to January 30: The day of arrest is not explicitly given anywhere. But since the tumult in the church of Zollikon falls on Sunday, January 29, we may surely assume that the arrest took place on Monday, January 30.

Page 46: Expulsion of the Augustinian hermits on December 3, 1524: see sources by W. Köhler, *Das Buch der Reformation Huldrych Zwingli's* (1926), p. 136 f.

Page 47: Zwingli develops his interpretation of Acts 19 in *Von der Taufe, von der Wiedertaufe und von der Kindertaufe,* 1525 (Critical Zwingli edition, Vol. IV, p. 282 f., and *Zwingli, Hauptschriften,* Vol. II, p. 87 f.) and in *Commentarius de vera et falsa religione,* 1525 (Critical Zwingli edition, Vol. III, p. 871 f.). In *Commentarius,* Zwingli states explicitly that when the Zollikon Anabaptists had been asked for the Scriptural evidence for rebaptism, they had answered with Acts 19.

Page 49: The concession for private Bible study must have been given the Zollikon men orally.

Page 53: The declaration in No. 48 indicates that 200 persons were present "in the parlor" during the two meetings of Blaurock in Murer's house. This I hold to be improbable because of the size of the room. A farmer's parlor did not have room for so many people. Was it meant to be 20?

Page 53: That women were gripped by the revival in such a personal way that they stand up and request baptism is unusual for the Reformation period, and shows that within the Anabaptist movement women gained religious independence.

Page 55: The report of the performance of rebaptism on a Sunday in the Zollikon church seems at first glance untenable, but is after all not so incredible. For until the eighteenth century the pastors of Zollikon had their residence in Zurich, and on the Sunday that Schad baptized in the church pastor Billeter perhaps had already returned to Zurich. Furthermore, the Zollikon Anabaptists had (as Nos. 69 and 93 show) not a few non-baptistic sympathizers with them, and so they had a certain backing in the village. And finally we call attention to No. 313 in Emil Egli's *Actensammlung zur Geschichte der Zürcher Reformation* (1879), where it is reported that in 1521 an unknown Lutheran pastor wanted to preach in the church of Eglisau in the canton of Zurich. The local clergyman tried to prevent him. Then a man from the audience stepped up to the native pastor and said to him: "You will let him preach, for the church does not belong to you, but to the congregation." A similar feeling may have prevailed at that time in Zollikon. (Reference kindly indicated by Mr. Heinrich Hedinger, a teacher in Zurich.)

Pages 62-67: I have given further details connected with the chapter "The Prophets of Zollikon" in *Mennonitische Geschichtsblätter*, 1952, pp. 2-10, in which I used several references given by Dr. Gerhard Goeters in Bonn. Contrary to my study of 1952, I am now of the opinion that the "penance" procession should be placed in June, 1525. I base this on No. 74 in L. v. Muralt and W. Schmid. From this source (Council decision of June 12, 1525) we learn that the Council of Zurich expected this procession. Evidently the intention of the Zollikon prophets had been made known (by an informer?) to the Council before it was carried out.

Page 65: The Münster prophets Knipperdolling and Bockelson: *Die Wiedertäufer zu Münster 1534-35; Berichte, Aussagen und Aktenstücke,* edited by Klemens Löffler (1923), pp. 15 and 25 f.

Page 65: Cries of woe in Amsterdam: W. J. Kühler, *Geschiedenis der Nederlandsche Doopsgezinden,* Vol. I (1932), p. 176. (Reference kindly indicated by Dr. M. West, Oxford.)

Page 65: About Melchior Hofmann, see the summary article by Christian Neff in *Mennonitisches Lexikon* II (1931).

Page 66: The late Professor D. Wilhelm Goeters (Bonn) called my attention to a pamphlet of 1524 with the title: "Wee: Fünff vnd vyertzig wee. Aus den Propheten von dem wörtlin Ve. / genant, Was es bedeüt, auff die künfftige zeit So / yetzund das Wort Gots als wenig würckt bey / vnns menschen, Gemacht von D. S. / zu W. etc. M.D.XXiiij. (Kuczynski 2742. Panzer, Annalen II, 310, 2451). I am also indebted to Professor Goeters for the communication of the following saying by the astrologer Johann Lichtenberger: "He who does not die in 1523, nor decay in 1524, nor is stricken dead in 1525, he may speak of miracle."

Page 69: Bible readers from Zollikon: The Bible edition which the readers of Zollikon used was Luther's translation. Three reprintings of Luther's New Testament came out in Zurich in 1524 (by Froschauer and Hager). In Basel, Luther's translation of the Old Testament was reprinted in 1523 and 1524 (by Petri), to the extent that it had been completed. A separate Zurich Bible translation did not exist at that time.

Page 72: Death of Zollikon Anabaptists at Kappel: see H. Bruppacher und Alex. Nüesch: *Das alte Zollikon* (1899), p. 81.